YOU ARE NOT ALONE

APRIL J. FORD

You Are Not Alone: How To Rise Above Life's Challenges With Grace, Gratitude, Love& Joy

By

April J. Ford

Crescendo Publishing, LLC
300 Carlsbad Village Drive
Ste. 108A, #443
Carlsbad, California 92008-2999
Cover Design by Melodye Hunter

ISBN: 978-0-9960761-3-5 (p)
ISBN: 978-0-9960761-4-2 (e)

A Message from the Author...

Click on the vide or the link to hear a personal message from April J. Ford, Author of You Are Not Alone: How To Rise Above Life's Challenges With Grace, Gratitude, Love & Joy

http://youtu.be/4YZb-TWpALg

To further support you on your journey, remember to download your free bonus gifts, including a free Companion Journal:

http://www.joysofyah.com/youarenotalonebookgifts/

April J Ford

Table of Contents

Introduction

———————— ≋ ————————

Was there ever a time when you felt you were overcompensating for your dreams, your values, your health, or more, only to realize the outcome of these compromises led to stress, weight gain, anxiety, fear, or even depression?

Maybe you put everyone else's needs before your own and discovered this compromise led you to feel alone?

Are you the mother who raised her family and who now finds herself—with her children grown—with no financial security, no loving relationship, and consumed with fear and worry?

Have you been suffering in silence and but don't know why?

Are you beautiful and fit on the outside, but, in reality, you're fighting internal emotional battles no one else can see?

Has life presented you with a challenge that has left you

feeling alone as you try to navigate where you're supposed to go?

If you said yes to any of this, YOU are not alone.

With all the roles we women play—wife, mother, sister, career climber, entrepreneur, and many more responsibilities with other titles—we run the risk of ignoring or diluting our health and wellness, our spiritualty, our parenting, our love and relationships, our happiness, and our success until these elements are disrupted or eventually destroyed.

The side effects of this destruction is causing an alarming rise in medicinal dependencies, suicides, domestic violence, abuse, neglect, divorces, disgruntled employees, anxiety, stress, depression, abandoned kids, poor academic performances in kids … and the list continues.

I am not blaming these side effects on women. Both genders within society must do our part to take ownership of responsibilities within our own family units and to create support within our communities for others.

Women must also learn to put themselves on their own to-do list. It's natural to us to nurture and nourish, but if YOU didn't even put yourself on the plan with everyone else to be taken care of, how can you expect anyone else to take care of you? You must acknowledge that you are worthy.

You'll find there are tons of books, seminars, coaches, and trainers out there teaching people how to be successful, happy, and wealthy, but what about when adversity hits? When your health, relationships, or finances are on the verge of destruction? When you were taking notes during that seminar on how to be successful or wealthy by having the right business plan, marketing strategy, or branding, did you hear them offer solutions for when you encounter adversity? Was that included in the plan? The secret ingredients to rising to any challenge—whether it's personal or business—is having grace, gratitude, love, and joy.

I will share with you real stories of experiences, emotions, and solutions for rising above life's challenges with grace, gratitude, love, and joy. I share my own personal stories, but I have also interlaced other people's stories with mine (although I have disguised them to protect their privacy as some of them are recognizable to the public eye). From these stories, you'll see how the *4 Step 4 R's Program* was used to create a blueprint for a renewed life when challenges arise.

When creating the 4 R's (Recognize, Respond, Reevaluate, Rebalance),my goal was to provide a simple, practical, and realistic method for navigating through adversity. It is simply organized in four steps:

1) RECOGNIZE the Rubble that needs to be cleared;
2) RESPOND with a Recovery plan on how to transition from tragedy to triumph;
3) REEVALUATE the plan as you Rebuild in alignment with your new journey for the future;
4) REBALANCE the relationships in your life that give you life.

The program is designed to work for anyone at any stage in his or her life. I've worked personally with leading industry experts (authors, media experts, fitness experts, celebrities, entrepreneurs, and more), and it is a powerful tool in the process of healing through adversity and moving toward an empowered life.

This book won't focus heavily on the 4 R's Program, but it will briefly reference it, particularly to offer examples as to how it can be integrated with real scenarios.

Here's an example of why I needed to rely on this program continually, as life didn't seem to be selfish when it came to handing out challenges or curveballs to me: I had a solid business plan written with the most qualified strategist. Attorneys that have represented major corporations even complimented the revision. But when certain personal factors such as my health, my relationship, and my finances all at once spun into a whirlwind, what good was that business plan? Do you think my marketing and branding strategy took priority? What would you do next? I had to figure it out. Although I tried to figure everything out on my own through trial and error, I felt alone during the process—until I started learning from other people. They too, were suffering in silence.

Before we go any further, I want to offer a transparent disclaimer: When I talk about love and relationships, I am no Marriage Family Therapist psychologist. When I talk about nutrition, I am not a nutritionist.(Actually, my degree is in electrical and electronic engineering.) I speak on various topics, from the grass-roots methods I used to learn on my own to learning from other experts. Think about it: How would those certifications or degrees framed on my wall serve you? Do you automatically become "certified," or would you want to hear from someone that's actually been living it as opposed to just studying it?

I didn't write my story because I became a widow at the age of thirty-two. My story actually began before this.

Although I'm going to relate events from my life or others, I believe you'll find a connection somewhere in your own journey.

Our journey called life is filled with happiness, success, fulfillment, disappointments, adversities, but all in all, blessings. The key to keep moving forward in your own path is finding gratitude first, even when there is contrast to the light. There is always gold to be found in life's challenges—it is the alchemy of adversity. (And when I refer to "alchemy," I'm referring to the metaphor of turning the rubble of metal into precious gold, not to the hocus-pocus of wizardry.)

You Are Not Alone, How To Rise Above Life's Challenges With Grace, Gratitude, Love & Joy is about finding the gold in life's challenges.

A path finding who we are inside and the way we handle the challenges we face is how we transition and transform into who we are truly meant to be. We are not only guided by our inner-self but the resources of guidance all around us, none of us are ever alone.

Becoming a widow at the age of thirty-two was a tragedy for me, but the challenges of all my prior adversities gave me the strength and foundation to transition from this tragedy to triumph. What sorts of adversities, you might ask.

My entire life was one loss after another. I lost my innocent childhood to my stepfather who molested me at a young age. I lost my respect for and trust in certain individuals who I felt failed to protect me. (I later forgave them, knowing it was their fear that overpowered them.) I lost my firstborn son to an adoption. I nearly lost my life twice, and then I did lose my husband suddenly.

One thing I never lost, though, was my faith. My faith fueled my dreams for a better life. We all have dreams for a reason. I had already lost so much in my lifetime; I wasn't going to lose my dreams.

Why am I sharing my story? I share my story so that others can share their stories and have their glory. I share my story so that others don't have to experience the extremities of what I faced but will be able to take the fruit of my adversities and prosper with it. I share my story to allow people to borrow my belief and faith. I share my love and light so that others can illuminate theirs. I share my joys and blessings so that others can share theirs, and to let others know, you are not alone.

"Every adversity has within it the seed of an equivalent or greater benefit." – Napoleon Hill

Dedication

You Are Not Alone is dedicated to my children who I leave my footprints for when my physical being is no longer here. I want them to learn that they will never be alone.

I also dedicate this publication to all those who seek; those who are seeking comfort, calmness, confidence, clarity and connection.

There is always gold to be found in life's challenges; it is the alchemy of adversity. Find yours and remember to share and spread your joys and blessings.

15
6 zeros
2-commas

RECOGNIZE THE RUBBLE

April J Ford

CHAPTER 1

Risks Of Over Compensating

———————≈———————

Can we as women have and do it all?

As women we've heard these names before: AlphaMom, SuperMom, Soccer Mom, Corporate Climber, and on and on. Just the title "Mom" itself represents many sub-roles: taxi-driver, counselor, financial planner, chef, housekeeper, family travel agent, nurse, gardener, personal shopper, etiquette expert, spiritual leader, party planner, dental hygienist, family cheerleader, homework regulator, etc., etc. ....

We're naturally wired to be a talented, multidimensional being—that's the beauty of our feminine energy. We're able to flow from one role to another. However, we must learn a very pivotal lesson that helps us to utilize this power within us called our light, which is the source of our energy. The feminine energy gives life and love; it nurtures growth. But oftentimes we tend to overcompensate and not realize our light needs to be replenished and nourished itself.

Where does the road lead us if we create a path by overworking too many hours a week as we climb the corporate ladder? What price do we pay for forging this path? What family and/or personal activities do we sacrifice as we pursue our career? Where does the road lead us when we create a path over committing our kids to so many extracurricular activities?

The symptoms of unrealistic expectations can include feeling overwhelmed and then overcompensating, which results in stress; weight gain; lack of sleep; unhealthy, addictive habits; unhealthy relationships; compromising our own worth and values; compromising our own dreams; depression; anxiety; meltdowns; and dependency on medications.

There is absolutely nothing wrong with "doing it all," with having a prosperous career, taking care of the household, and being a loving wife and nurturing mom. However, oftentimes we don't create boundaries, boundaries to learn how to say no to things that are not that important to our lives, boundaries based on what we value, boundaries that prevent self-imposed or external guilt from creeping in to make us feel bad when we give ourselves permission to take care of ourselves first. It's okay to give ourselves permission to be successful, and it's okay to create boundaries that allow only an inner circle near us who genuinely support and respect us.

Asking for help is okay. Actually, people naturally want to help you if they love or care about you. But sometimes people don't know how to offer their help.

I'll give you an example. I was at a friend's graduation celebration dinner one evening. My friend's husband started a conversation with me about how he and his son were just thinking about my son, and they thought of just picking him up one day to hang out "with the boys." Well, I asked him what happened since I never got that call. His reply was that they've always viewed me as having it all together and doing it all, so they assumed I didn't need help. My reply to him was, "What if I don't need help but instead want help...that counts." So my point is, just ask. Whether you're on the receiving or giving end, just ask. It really does take a village and a team to raise a child. Why not put people on your team that are willing to help? And don't forget to put God on your team.

"So I say to you, ask, and it will be given to you; seek, and you will find; knock, and it will be opened to you. For everyone who asks, receives; and he who seeks, finds; and to him who knocks, it will be opened."(Luke 11:9)

Perfection means making mistakes. It's okay to ask for help. It's okay to say no when your plate is already full, and it's okay to put you first (after God). It's not okay to overcompensate and compromise—our health, spirituality, family, relationships, happiness, and success.

Statistics from PewResearch have shown that the roles of the mothers and fathers in the home are converging when it comes to the responsibilities of child care and housework because there are more women in the workforce. Both mothers and fathers find it difficult to manage all the responsibilities, and this is coming from a dual-parent household. You can only imagine the weight of responsibility a single parent bears. These difficulties can have a domino effect if not addressed properly; being overstressed can strain relationships, create health issues, and even impact your performance at work.

Washington Post writer Brigid Schulte and author of *Overwhelmed, Work, Love and Play When No One Has the Time* did an interview on KPCC Radio (Southern California Public Radio http://youtu.be/t6A_lIWvv6g), and I recall her making a statement that basically pointed me out specifically. She said that people's perception of leisure had to be tied to an element of productivity, as if we don't believe we deserve leisure. I felt like she was pointing at me because it was extremely difficult for me to grasp the idea of rest; I made it difficult on my end. I admit that I can be a "busy body" multitasking. It was a self-sabotaging thought that I always had to be doing something to be productive. I'll share a perfect example from *Chase the Challenge and Conquer* that illustrates overcompensating and neglecting the value and importance of resting, which provides recovery and restoration.

Shortly after becoming a widow, I decided to mow the lawn. I guess this was the superwoman syndrome. I felt like I had to pick up both roles in the household, those I performed and those my husband performed. I knew how to operate the lawnmower, but I guess on this particular day it decided to test my persistence and patience and refused to start. I ended up rupturing a vein in my wrist wrestling with it.

The next day I went to urgent care to make sure my wrist was okay, and the visit ended with me having a nervous breakdown in the lobby as I waited my turn to be called. I had no business fussing with the lawn mower and should have been home just resting and calling on help to take care of the lawn. I wasn't responding well to the urgent care environment because my husband had passed fairly recently at the hospital next door. The dialogue in my head was something like, "What am I doing here? I don't want to be here again. I don't want to go through what I just went through." There I was, supposedly going in to have my wrist examined, and I ended up getting rushed into the exam room for an EKG, X-rays, and lab work because I was about to faint in my own sweat sitting in the lobby. I should have asked for help. I should have rested.

Ask yourself if the daily burnout is worth the negative effects on your marriage. Is it worth diluting or deleting your own dreams as you fuel and build everyone else's dreams—both at home and work? Are you so drained that you have nothing else to give but complaints?

Rest really is underrated. Do the doctors who prescribe that we should get eight hours of sleep per night even get their sleep, when they are the ones working twelve or sixteen hour days?!We don't get enough sleep as it is, and our perception of leisure has to be tied to an element of productivity as Schulte explained. The science of our body is that it's constantly operating whether we are asleep or awake. Certain parts of our bodies have peak performance times and need time for repair and restoration, such as the cells in our heart, liver, stomach, etc. When we create an internal ecosystem of being burned out and stressed, when we lack nutrition, how is the body supposed to optimally function?

If you're overcompensating and compromising, you're living a life in survival mode. We all have survival phases, but why not design your life to thrive? There's a difference between surviving and thriving. Thriving means you wake up energized and excited about what you're going to be working on. You have a sense of happiness and fulfillment. You are more efficient with your time and can volunteer at your child's school or give to your community. Others love being around you because you operate at a higher vibrational frequency and your energy radiates. You know what your life means. You're able to imagine your future self staring at you today, smiling at you today because you designed your life based on your vision. This is what it's like to thrive!

God didn't give us a purpose to be miserable, and he definitely didn't give us life to be unhappy. This is not to say that everything will come with ease and no adversity, but why not choose the positive path where we can prosper and thrive? Be honest and true to yourself about what fulfills you and makes you happy. Be honest about your definition of success. As women we tend to be people-pleasers, but we are not the designers of other peoples' lives, only ours; we can aid and assist, but we are not their designers.

If you are or were in the workforce, what were some other challenges that you faced? Did you have to debate taking maternity leave when giving birth to your child and going back to work immediately to secure your position among your peers? Were you in a field that was predominately populated by men, which added an extra layer of competition among the other women in your environment? Did you have the proper mentorship and leadership support from other women? Was your company cognizant of retaining women in the workforce and being able to adapt and be flexible to the demands of having a work-life balance?

To briefly touch on a topic that's self-evident and poses unnecessary challenges, why are women more critical or competitive of other women? Are they insecure and intimidated that someone's brightness will over-shine theirs? If we only realize how much we can empower each other by being less destructive towards each other, the advancement of women in society can make a positive impact globally. Aside from being responsible and executing to all the roles listed above, women are given a gift from God and tend to be naturally compassionate, emotionally understanding, and nurturing— all what the world needs more of.

For me, I was really surprised and disappointed when I lost my husband and was given only three days of bereavement leave. Thankfully I had an awesome manager who fought for me with the HR department and got more than just three days! After all, the darn autopsy itself took almost a year. Now, you would think that since my husband and I had both worked with this company for many years and since they were publicly promoting the retention of technical minority women in the workforce, this would have been the perfect storm for them to show their support without resistance.

Although we as women are talented multidimensional beings, these are realistic challenges that are becoming an epidemic in our society and our households. Having too many roles and responsibilities without boundaries compromises our health, worthiness, value and values, relationships, etc.

Hearing stories from other women, I see a pattern of how they've lived their entire lives for other people. This is beautiful, but if you do not put yourself first, the ramifications of overcompensating in the end will present greater challenges. These women spent all their years raising their kids and caring for their husbands, putting the needs of their families before their own.

One woman went through a long divorce. The husband took the house, and she was left with all the kids and no financial support. All her income went to raising the kids and left her with no retirement by the time the kids were adults.

Another lady raised three beautiful kids on her own, but later in life, when her kids were sufficiently in their own careers, she had to redefine herself in the marketplace to earn a living. All her savings, investments, retirement, and time went into her children.

I'm not saying we should fall short with our responsibilities as mothers and wives. I simply want to bring awareness to the fact that you need to set up a foundation where you are part of the equation to be taken care of—financially, health wise, etc.

Who wants to be in their seventies before they start "living" because that's when the government says you can retire? Who even gave us the authority to say we are guaranteed a tomorrow, let alone a time in the future called our retirement age; heck my husband was "young, fit and healthy". Who wants to worry about entering the marketplace to redefine your skill sets, or put the burden on your own kids to take care of you because YOU didn't put YOU on the plan to be taken care of?

In addition to creating boundaries, we must learn how to harness the power of our feminine energy. We all have both forms of energy—male and female. The male energy is typically more task-oriented, goal-driven, and compartmentalized compared with the feminine energy that is more creative and free-flowing as a whole. More details on this topic are outlined in the Spirituality section on the importance of and impact to our health and well-being.

Are you able to recognize the symptoms in your life and know what they mean? Is your body telling you that it has hit a plateau with your workouts? Is it fatigued from the lack of sufficient rest and proper nutrition? Are you lacking focus and motivation? These are all indicators/symptoms that your internal system is trying to tell you something; your system is under stress, lacking something, and ultimately there's an imbalance somewhere.

"Put YOU back on your own To-Do List."

April J Ford

RESPOND WITH A RECOVERY PLAN

CHAPTER 2

Health & Wellness

———— ≈ ————

For many of us women, we tend to put our own health and wellness on the back burner behind others' needs. The reality is, without our own sound health, we can be nothing to ourselves, let alone to others.

I must admit that even when I was with my book strategist and business coach, brainstorming the format of this book that you're reading now, I had to eat my own words. I was going to move the "Parenting" section of this book above the order of priority for "Health & Wellness." Then I caught myself, saying, "Oops, I guess I'm just like my audience." Here, even I demonstrated that I should put my kids before my own wellness. But again, the reality is, what good am I—how am I going to provide for them—if my health is not sound? I recall a time when I was extremely sick and had to go to the doctor. On that day when I wasn't able to function, I had to rely on five or six other people for my household to operate: picking up and dropping off kids for school, driving me to the doctor, cooking dinner.... The list went on and on.

The misconception or excuse many of us have is, "I don't have time." Well, I would encourage you to measure the time you're actually short-changing yourself when you don't make time for your health. Would you rather have critical, nonreversible, detrimental effects later down the road? Or would you rather take daily measures—making even minor adjustments—and integrate them into your existing lifestyle? Would you agree that doing a quick twenty-minute activity per day would yield some sort of benefit, especially when compared to accumulated years with no activity? Weight gain, high blood pressure, heart disease—we've all seen the statistics on the leading causes of death.

Don't let the little voice of guilt start a dialog in your head. Don't let it convince you that just because you're working out or conscious of what you eat that you're being selfish.

Through my journey of health and healing, I have adopted both Eastern and Western modalities. (I discuss these topics in more depth in the spiritually section.) I've explored various methods that I believe worked for me, such as sound therapy, breathing exercises, body talk, meditation, reiki, crystal therapy, and essential oils, just to name a few.

You might hear some opposition or controversy when it comes to nontraditional methods. Some radicals may go so far as to call these practices demonic or hocus-pocus when they don't realize that God sees the intention behind the practices of the action. For example, one might argue and ask if it's okay for Christians to drink wine during communion as a symbol of Jesus' blood, what about cults that perform their own blood rituals? Again, it is the intention behind the action. If someone lights a candle for aromatherapy, does that mean they are summoning demon spirits?

Crystals have also had their share of controversy in this realm. Crystals have been used in technologies such as cell phones, computers, watches, etc. So we can use the crystals to advance our technologies and monetize a product, but when it comes to its natural healing purposes to realign energy flow, it is frowned upon? Essential oils have been used for healing purposes, and they are referenced in the Bible. I've been using sound therapy; others call it Soul Song or Spirit Song (from my own Transformational Expert and Spiritual Coach, Wendy, who created *Healing Harmonics*). I have seen and felt its incredible beauty but most importantly its results.

I won't unpack the science here, but you can research Dr. Leonard Horowitz's work on the divine frequency of 528 representing God's creation of Love and God's language of math. Dr. Horowitz also teaches the relationship of the Bible to the crystalline forms in water. Again, crystals are electromagnetic receivers and transmitters holding the frequency and memory for healing. The frequency of 528 is known as the love-miracle frequency that repairs damaged DNA. That is why it is the blueprint of life. Love heals.

"These original sound frequencies were apparently used in the great Hymn to St. John the Baptist that, along with many Gregorian chants, were lost centuries ago according to church officials. The chants and their special tones were believed to impart special spiritual blessings when sung in harmony during religious masses."– See more at:

http://www.528records.com/pages/dna-repair-frequency-revealed-bible-intrigues-scientists-and-religious-scholars#sthash.bk8ltqwS.dpuf

Here's a clue as to how to unlock your DNA and provide longevity…love and healthy water! So there really is nothing new under the sun. Through my adversities, I learned that finding the strength of love in my heart supported my faith and courage with grace, gratitude, and joy.

I'll share a story of how silly I felt when I decided to test my commitment. At this point in my learning of healing modalities and meditation, I was already familiar with crystals, so performing this test was probably just for my ego. I was on a spiritual retreat in Moab, Utah, and I was staying at Sorrel Ranch. (You might be familiar with the ranch and surrounding areas as it's been featured in so many movies and commercials.)I was reading the *Crystal Bible* one evening and came across the part where it talks about how the energy of the crystals "speak" or vibrate to each person. So I pulled out a row of crystals and looked at each one, "listening" to which one I should pick up. I picked one up and then looked up the meaning of this particular crystal. Well, let's just say that the healing properties of this crystal all had to do with what my meditation was about earlier in the day with my spiritual coach Tammy. I also did this another time when I picked up a certain crystal and just kept it near my work area. When I looked up the properties of this particular crystal, I thought it was pretty funny that it matched what my Zyto scan and Body Talk session had focused on (more about Zyto and Body Talk later).

I've learned to honor and to stop trying to figure everything out and appreciate what's already been given by our Creator to heal ourselves—even the knowledge he gives us to advance and combine both traditional Western medicine and Eastern practices. From the water, light, sound, color, air, and words, all things go back to the form of energy, and energy comes from THE light. Yes, words have power. When you speak the thought that formed that word, you are creating vibrational energy to give it life. Your breath gave it life, and the sound vibrating in the air transmits an energy field. Have you heard of the saying, "Prayer can go places you can't"? Our Creator created everything from energy, and he sees all energy. Some Western traditionalists may call this hocus-pocus, but knowing the TRUTH is all that really matters.

If these modalities are foreign to you, I would recommend getting a Zyto scan to start. I was at a personal development seminar in San Diego, and they had a health and wellness section. One of the demos was for a Zyto scan, but I was a little suspicious of this small, hand cradle contraption.

The scan is basically a biofeedback mechanism and allows you to view how the energy in your body is functioning, which affects how your body functions, including your stomach, heart, digestive system, etc. When I had my first scan, I was quite impressed with its accuracy. I compared my results with the results I received from other naturopathic holistic practitioners (who knew nothing about Zyto technology), and they were in alignment.

Health and wellness means having a HEALTHY MIND, a HEALED BODY, and a HAPPY SOUL. I encourage you to read the section in the *4 Step 4 R's Program* describing a realistic approach to what's healthy to maintain depicted by "The Real Before Picture."Keep in mind what's healthy in all aspects—mental, emotional, and physical.

I'll share a small portion here so that you'll see how our emotions affect our health. After competing in a fitness show, I gained at least twenty-five to thirty pounds because I was eating out of deprivation and stress, and in response to my emotions.

The Real Before Picture

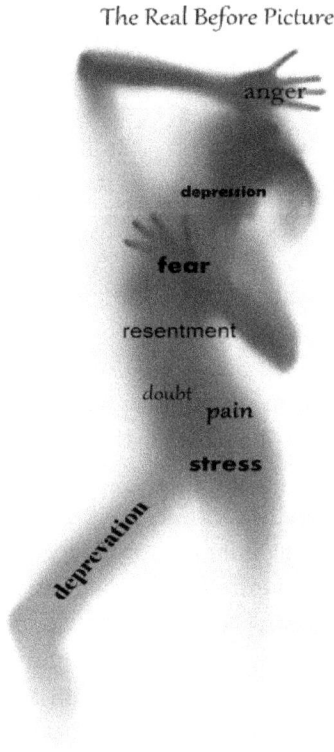

Some may say that my twenty-five to thirty pounds of weight gain were just "vanity pounds," but to me, I didn't like how I felt or looked. Most importantly, though, what I really _felt and looked like inside_ is depicted by this picture. I call it my real "before" picture. This was the real before picture—before my fitness show—because it eventually revealed itself after the show, when the weight gain stemmed from deprivation, stress, and emotions (some may be new emotions, while others were already present and hadn't been addressed).

To explain this picture, I was holding onto anger and fear, shying away from and denying depression, carrying resentment, feeling doubt/anxiety (the kind you feel in your stomach), and so on. After sharing this part of my story, many women who were also suffering in silence came to be honest about their emotions and actions and decided to share their experiences.

The state of your emotions and feelings stem from your perception and thoughts. What you perceive is what you believe. What you believe affects your decisions and the actions you take after you make a decision.

With my share of adversities, I've learned that a positive mindset helps me persevere through any rubble. Later on, I learned about Napoleon Hill's principles on personal development, including having a positive mental attitude. I guess when adversity hits our path, we have to take the fast track to survival and figure things out pretty quickly. So why not learn from what you're reading here—and from others—so that you can prevent as much adversity as possible and shrink the timeframe to your happiness and success.

Your life can be challenging or you can learn the power your thoughts have when it comes to conquering life's adversities. Whatever you perceive, you believe; whatever you believe, you make decisions on; and your decisions lead you to your actions. You are where you are today in your life because of the actions you've taken on the decisions you've made. The grace and exception I would give is when either evil takes over a person's free will, and their capacity to realize they were influenced was swept away from them because of their weakness, or when an unexpected adversity hits.

Perceive - >Believe - > Decision -> Actions

When I transitioned from an engineer to an entrepreneur, I focused on personal development. I've always loved to read, but this growing process was more than just reading books. It was attending seminars; participating in networking events; listening to audio books; practicing affirmations daily; creating visuals for my goals; dream building (immersing myself in the environment I was targeting); continuing my spiritual growth through mentorship, retreats, and learning other modalities; and most importantly, developing relationships with people who were further along in the process than I was embarking upon and increasing my desire to get to know God better in my life. This does not mean I was one of those people that read the Bible cover to cover everyday. Frankly, I've been guilty in the past of reading the Bible like it's a dictionary. Why a dictionary? You only go to it when you need to look something up—and some people don't even use it.

Going to events or seminars can be a game changer for someone's life, but it's the "meeting after the meeting" where you'll reap what you sow.

Think of how great it is to not only hear phenomenal pioneers and leaders on stage such as the person who invented "xyz" or the person who went from ground zero to not only multimillions but to billions of dollars. Just being in the same room with them inspires you, but to be able to share a meal with them, to learn their pearls of wisdom and golden nuggets, to have them genuinely support your business, or maybe just to develop the relationship and connection to be able to appreciate what they have accomplished and contributed to the world with their efforts, those are priceless experiences.

Oftentimes I've even made connections to relay an introduction to others so that they can collaborate with their efforts. I've found this law to be constant and consistent: when you're coming from a place of serving people first, your needs and more will always be blessed. You'll just have to do your research on which events and seminars serve you best and how you serve that population best as well. It can get costly with the admission tickets, travel, and "back of the room sales." Some events are just to hype you up. As Dani Johnson (best-selling author and success coach) called it, "Giving you milk, but what about the meat?" She meant although you are all in a positive environment, encouraging one another to believe or be successful, what practical tools are you getting out of the event that you can implement to yield similar results?

One thing I have noticed, you should be aware of those who are truly there to serve, whether as an attendee or a featured speaker. Yes, everyone should network at events, but people should network discreetly and professionally. Don't impose your product or services on someone else if it doesn't mutually benefit you both.

Many speakers I have found are there just to promote themselves. At one event, I sat in the back of the room observing the attendees. Although most of them were entrepreneurs just getting started in their businesses, they had invested a lot of time, effort, and resources to get where they were, and I commended them for that. But the thoughts going through my head as I listened to the speaker on stage were that, this crowd already had enough information to get them to their next milestone of goals. What they're lacking is either the right contact or the funds to get them there. As I continued to listen, the speaker offered only their story of adversity and how they will offer their time to coach. This is not to dilute the value of the speaker's time nor their results they've gained, but if they are truly there to serve, why not tithe their time of coaching? Or why not pick up their phone to make a connection happen, or maybe even gift the other person with funds?

For the entrepreneur, work with what you have; start with that and work on what's next. I'm a big proponent of investing in personal development. Just be cautious. Don't get caught up in going to events and bombarding yourself with information overload and end up not doing anything with it. You also don't want to use your funds on all these products. (I'm sure they're all great since they came from success stories that worked, but what did you do with it?)Think about what you need now and what you need next. I'm sure the resources are all within your existing contacts.

Mentorship and coaching can come in two forms, formal or informal. Formal means you have a direct connection with them; informal means when you're studying their work and/or attending their events, you see them as a role model but you have no direct contact. Formal can also mean that you're in constant and consistent contact with your mentor or that you just have a casual, ongoing relationship with them. You can make the most of any of these situations. Some of the people I've met at events I've only seen on stage, some I've connected with afterwards, some I've developed a constant contact with, and some were just a one-time connection. The point is you should always expand your awareness and think about what you can learn from them.

I still remember the first time I saw best-selling author from *The Secret*, John Assaraf, speak at a conference. He was talking about his Daily Method of Operation, his "DMO." These are activities you are doing on a daily basis that are considered "income-producing activities."

We all have the same twenty-four hours in a day, but how is it that successful people are able to have more money and more time? He also talked about how he leveraged his strengths and hired his weakness. My point is, in this example Assaraf would be an indirect mentor/coach for me since I haven't had the privilege yet to actually interact with him directly. On the other hand, I've connected with other mentors/coaches directly, either on a consistent basis or occasionally when our paths intersect.

I've gotten to know another best-selling author, inventor, and advisor, David Corbin, and we had a discussion about my uniqueness, strengths, and weakness. In his book *Illuminate – Harnessing the Positive Power of Negative Thinking*, he describes his approach, which is that we should accentuate the positive while tackling the negative. I fully embrace his concept; we should leverage our strengths, but it is our weaknesses, our negatives, that are going to prevent us from closing the gaps on our wins and victories.

In one of my previous blogs, "Ricochet Back At Life," I recall an Olympic track and field athlete saying that he was able to accomplish winning because he trained to improve his weak areas. This provided a balance that made him a stronger athlete and a better competitor, which makes sense because if we think about it, if his strength was speed but his weakness was an injury, would his strength win the race then?

"Healthy Mind, Healed Body, Happy Soul"

April J Ford

CHAPTER 3

Spirituality

———— ≈ ————

What does spirituality mean to you? Do you resonate more with defining it as an internal experience or participating in organized religion?

I will share my opinions based on my own experiences. I would define it in these forms: being able to tap into your own internal spirit/your soul through various methods, such as prayer, meditation, yoga, praise, worship; reading the Bible; working out; or just being still to create a direct connection with our Creator.

Why is spirituality important?

"We are spiritual beings having a human experience." – Pierre Teilhard de Chardin

Although our current society is going through a spiritual awakening phase where more individuals are being activated with their internal frequencies, it is still not widely accepted or common knowledge that we are not only human beings but also spiritual beings. It is imperative that we operate in all three of our beings: mind, body, and soul. It is the only way we can successfully operate in cohesion as a collective consciousness.

The practices that enable us to connect with our soul, such as meditation, prayer, worship, etc., provide many benefits. Prayer can bring strength and comfort; meditation leads to positive thoughts, actions, and an overall sense of well-being, which all translate to energizing and nourishing your soul. Breathing through these practices reduces stress, increases energy, elevates moods, provides cleansing and clarity, and so much more.

To me, prayer and meditation are two different practices. Yes, both enable you to connect with your soul, but in prayer, I can directly communicate with God through spirit. Meditation is a self-reflection. Both bring a deeper meaning and feeling of fulfillment and connection to your own higher purpose.

There are many meditation guides to aid the "how-to" process of meditating, but there is no one clear, universal instruction set for everyone on how to direct our minds since we are all different. I encourage you to start with something to aid you, but it can only be accomplished through personal practice. Some may like to listen to music while others want no music. Others may like to be in nature while others prefer to be indoors.

Growing through spiritual awakening provides a transformational experience through the transition process and results in healing. One must realize that the process is a **trans**ition before it becomes trans**form**ational. You can't "form" anything without a process ("trans"–going through/across) first. The formation comes after as a result.

I had this realization through my own process of awakening my spiritual side that provided immense healing within. If you can reflect for a moment on a particular time when you were facing an adversity, didn't that moment come crashing down with a drastic change already in your life? Did you lose a spouse through a death or divorce? Did you lose custody of your child? Did you lose a job? Did the doctor put a timestamp on your life? Well, any adversity presents a pretty drastic change in ones' being. Do you think you were, at this particular moment, open to hearing the word *transformation*?

Transformation represents a drastic change; I would suspect it's the last thing you'd want in the moment of adversity. Transition, however, provides a navigation through peace, security, stability, answers, and healing.

Different people seek various methods to aid in their transition process: a counselor, a physiatrist, spiritual healer, medical doctor, etc.

If you haven't been awakened, and you're asking why this is important, that's okay. We're all human beings, but it is not taught or recognized (for the most part) in our society that we are spiritual beings too. I think mankind has tried to be at top of the hierarchy of creation and formulate conclusions on our existence. For my personal beliefs, I don't need to prove my Creator, God.

So why is it important to recognize this part of our being, our spirituality? Because we were all created to have a life destined for happiness and success? In your spirituality! Do you think it's manufactured with the thoughts in your mind—whether you created the thoughts or you were exposed to them? Where did the thoughts and perceptions come from? Consider my example: I went to college for a BS in EEE and had a career with the top semi-conductor company in the world for fourteen years and later found out it wasn't my definition of happiness and success. I basically went to school for this degree on the sound advice of my family because it was the industry where the money was. Of course, I was grateful for the opportunity and experience with this career.

We must all establish skills and be able to provide for our living, but at least be aware of who you are and who you are meant to be. When you tap into this part of your being, then you'll feel fulfilled and your life will prosper on your own terms—not someone else's definition of what success should look like for you. Spirituality allows you to be connected to your Creator so that you are aligned with your purpose. It provides clarity, validation, nourishment, peace, and joy. It's like having access to the Creator that wrote the blueprint of your life. I do believe that we each have our destinies mapped out, but we also have freewill on how to get there, and that's where we get to design our own life. We travel toward our own destiny directed by God, but since we have freewill, sometimes our human self creates confusion or conflict. It's easy to let God do the work, but the willingness to surrender is not the easy part. For me, I created a saying for myself, *"God, show me the way and I'll obey."* But trust me, that had to come with practice and repeating to myself, *"Let Go, Let God, God Got Me!"*

If you haven't concluded yet the importance of your spiritual being as it relates to your higher purpose and being able to connect within and with your Creator, let's look at another significant importance.

As previously discussed in the Risk of Overcompensating Section, each of our beings consists of both the male and female energy. The male energy trends more (not always) on the left brain to be logical and linear thinking, compared with the female energy that trends more (again, not always) on the right side to be emotional and creative. How effective would it be to completely operate on the far extent of rational thinking without being mindful of your own or others' feelings? On the other hand, when being too emotional, our thinking can be hindered and impaired.

Learning how to meditate can provide help as you practice finding a flow of both energies to maintain a harmonious whole. This allows for the energy to be realigned with the body. Oftentimes, when there are blockages or imbalances of energy, there are disruptions that can be harmful to our physical body, emotional state, and mental health. The alignment of our physical, mental, emotional, and spiritual states are imperative to the core of our wellness. Many people often ask me what I eat, what workouts I do, and how I stay motivated to be healthy. My answer is simple: I just made it a habit to a point where it comes naturally to me. Oftentimes we have to create new behavioral (neuroscience) patterns to break a bad habit, and eventually it will turn into a habit.

"...the secret of how to break the power of hypnotic rhythm is wrapped in the seven principles...two most effective devices for mastering human beings are the habit of drifting and the law of hypnotic rhythm." from Napoleon Hill's *Outwitting The Devil – The Secret to Freedom and Success.*

EquiSync® (http://eocinstitute.org/meditation/) isa brainwave technology used for meditation. The effects of brainwave patterns that directly correlate to our thoughts and moods and our mental and emotional states of mind have been studied. The power of meditation has been seen to reduce and even reverse illnesses.

A close friend of mine (Sarah) saw the value of

understanding our brainwave states—Alpha, Beta, Delta, Theta—and invented Somadome (www.somadome.com). Somadome is a meditation pod that guides your breathing patterns through meditations. These binaural beats create the brainwave patterns. In the Health & Wellness Section, we touched on the topics of frequencies from crystals. In the pod, there are crystalline tiles that resonate frequencies to allow your energy within to flow freely. The Somadome also integrated the concept of color therapy. Color is formed from the wavelengths of light; this form of energy affects living cells.

As you can see by now, spirituality coincides with health and wellness. Sound, breathing, brainwave patterns, vibrational energy, and frequencies are all the spiritual tools and DNA decoders that our Creator already gave us to allow for healing.

Many may be confused by or have conflicts reading this section, and that's okay. With all the nonsense programming we constantly receive subconsciously through what we see on TV, hear on the radio, read on billboards, and even the foods we eat, all this affects our neuropathways that shape our belief system.

Your spiritual side is always there. It's like a seed in the dirt, but it needs to be fertilized and nourished in order for it to grow.

Now that you understand what spirituality is, some of the methods used through the transition process of awakening, as well as the benefits, lead into the transformational phase. At this stage you are open, ready, and equipped to receive guidance. It's like the radio in your car; the antenna is constantly picking up the broadcast being transmitted, but if you don't know how to tune your station or what station to tune it to, you are not going to receive the signal. Once your frequencies are tuned to the right station, you will get the message that you are not alone. All this time the guidance has been there, but your antennas weren't properly tuned to the right frequency to receive it.

A paradigm shift is occurring with people's beliefs and perception of what it really means to be spiritual and spiritual beings. I have found that the more in tune I was with my intuitive channel, the clearer life flowed. Divine guidance is already within us. Have you heard the phrase, "God works through people"? Well, those people are guided as much as you are.

There have been so many instances where I've been guided spiritually and by others who were guided and led to connect with me at a particular pivotal moment. There is no science that can explain divine intervention or guidance. I'm glad (for my mind's sake of sanity) that a few of these instances were recorded on audio. In the most unexpected times we'll get guidance; not all blessings are disguised. It is in the form of **boldwords** for confirmations, written in black and white as you see here, painted in your dreams, or sometimes even the whispers you hear spoken louder than words.

I recall a couple occasions, I was preparing an agenda for a one-on-one business-coaching meeting. I thought I had come so prepared. Let's just say that the conversations at each of these meetings took a U-turn and basically put the agenda on low priority. These separate meetings with different people at different times brought tears to my eyes because they were messages I needed to hear. I recall at one of them I even asked with puzzlement, "Who are you?!"

You'll get to a point where you graciously receive all the good God sends your way, without question. You will just receive it with a smile of gratitude and acknowledge that he is looking out for you. For example, I was in San Diego and Orange County looking for possible areas to live. People called me suddenly, and out of the blue. How did they know to call me at that particular moment in time? How did they know where I was? It's like having guardian angels by your side helping to direct you.

I don't know about you, but I want to receive guidance from an infinite intelligence, especially when we cannot lean on our own understanding to figure everything out during trials of adversity. I challenge you to expand your awareness. Think of great people you admire whether they are famous or not. Did they face an adversity before they got to where they are today? Most likely so. Do they share an element of awareness and spiritual consciousness? Most likely so. It's almost like a spiritual rite of passage where you humble your human, egotistic self and honor your spiritual being. My point is, your fears, doubts, worry, and pain inflicted by a challenge may cause you to feel alone, but when you allow yourself to believe the truth, your discovery toward spiritual freedom unlocks and reveals that God is real and heaven is here.

"Treat life like a GPS. You must know your desired destination before your turn-by-turn directions. Remember to use your internal compass called intuition as well."

RE-EVALUATE WHAT YOU'RE REBUILDING

CHAPTER 4

Defining Your Own Success & Happiness

————— ≈ —————

Are you willing to do what it takes to succeed? It's called failing! But the good news is, if you learn from others' mistakes and failures, you can collapse your timeframe for success.

You've already come to realize that even after obtaining financial success—money, homes, cars, etc.—your spirit is still unsettled. This is because you are worth "more" than that. The "more" part can be revealed, earned, and achieved only when we are walking in accordance with our true potential and purpose. The "more" does not constitute acquiring more things.

It wasn't always so even for me. People thought my story started when I became a widow at thirty-two years old since all they saw before that was a happy marriage, beautiful kids, a successful, six-figure engineering career, a well-stamped passport, cars, houses, and parties. But they didn't know about the journey through adversities I had to endure, even at a young age, to get to all of those things. What they also didn't know and see was that my spirit was unsettled and resettling with a knowledge that I had a deeper meaning, a deeper passion and purpose to life.

All of those things I accomplished were in my picture of what success looked like, but as I grew more toward fulfillment as opposed to acquirement, I defined success and happiness with a different picture.

God gave me a dream, just as he gave you yours and everyone else's. Expect no one to understand your vision completely because it is only for you. Others may support you in guiding you, but it's your vision.

Oftentimes people settle and forget about their dreams. Dani Johnson said it best: *"98% of the population shrink their dreams to fit their income. Meanwhile, the 2% find ways to increase their income so they can make their dreams happen."* This means people settle for their current circumstances or comfort zone. I wonder if people ever thought about why they gave up on their dreams when God, the dream giver, never gave up on them.

For me, it was harder to leave my dream than it was to leave my comfort zone. Staying in the corporate world, for me, would mean suppressing and leaving my dreams behind. That to me was a greater loss than the loss of my comfort zone and security of the pay and benefits. Although I'm extremely grateful for the opportunity, skills, and people I met throughout my corporate career, it was just a transition phase for me. I either inspired people when I walked away from a successful career because they wanted to do the same and didn't have the same courage, or they thought I was crazy because I was a widow with two kids risking the security of what the job provided. Stepping out of my comfort zone, I did feel discomfort, fear, and a self-awareness of my lack of skills in certain areas to fulfill my dream, but one thing I did have was my FAITH WAS GREATER THAN MY FEAR!

"Now faith is the substance of things hoped for, the evidence of things not seen." (Hebrews 11:1)

Picture yourself sitting on the shoreline of a beach charting your next sailing journey through life. You're calculating the sunrise and sunset times, when the tide is high and low, and even the wind. Some people spend so much time calculating instead of just implementing that the next thing you know, the sun has risen and set for many days. The days turn into weeks, months, and years. When will you go out there in the blue ocean to actually sail? It is only then you'll experience life and be able to adjust with the tides and wind; you can't get anywhere from the shoreline. No plan is ever perfect; the only way to test it is to put it in action and make the adjustments and modifications as you sail through your journey. Even if you put only one piece or a part of your plan into action, at least there's energy being put forth to bring it to life. Without energy, there will be no life, no fruition. Not everything is going to go according to what's in the plan, and something will come up that wasn't even part of the plan.

Notice I did mention the tides and winds you'll encounter when pursuing your dreams, your goals, your passion, or even your calling. Don't have a misconception that just because you were ordained to become someone that the waters are going to automatically part wherever you cast your vision or that you will meet no resistance or opposition.

Key secrets to avoid failure:

- Be persistent. People have a misconception that failing is when you act upon something and don't meet the expected results, when in fact true failure is just giving up or not even trying. The real obstacle here is that people fear not being able to attain the end results they desire, so they don't even try. Fear is a big inhibiter to success. **Fear motivates failure.** People fear the unknown path; unknown results; their unknown abilities; being judged, accepted, or ridiculed. People fear just the fear of failure itself!

- Since we are human and susceptible to flaws and imperfections, we are allowed to fail. None of us are perfect and immune to failure. But remember there is an option to get back up again. I call this "ricocheting back at life."

- Don't set yourself up for failure by setting unrealistic expectations. Only you know yourself better than anyone else.

- If you don't know how to get to your goals, seek help from experts.

- Acknowledge each incremental change. Your positive inner thoughts and gratitude toward yourself will keep you fueled and motivated. Remember this is a process. Create a daily routine/schedule; however, have a backup plan so that you can be fluid with unexpected changes.

Your plan and God's plan for you may vary to certain degrees. I call this the "Army Rule of Protection." God doesn't want to draw everything out on a plan and put it in a soldier's (your) pocket because when they get captured, they've now just compromised the plan and the soldier's safety. God gives us some parts of our plan (through our intuition) for direction but only enough for what we need.

This is to protect us when we fall into environments, situations, circumstances, and predicaments that were not part of the master plan.

I know it takes a leap of faith to listen to your intuition and to honor your calling. Bruce Wilkinson in *The Dream Giver: Following Your God-Given Destiny*, said, *"Comfort is the biggest enemy of your Dream. There's nothing the matter with wanting to be comfortable. But ultimately, Dreams are to help someone else. Comfort is to help yourself."*

I give you permission to borrow from my faith, syphon my belief and dreams until you have yours. I give you permission to dream again, believe again, share your dreams, share your passions, and most importantly share your gifts! Each of us has an ordained gift that is not to be withheld but to be shared. One of the reasons I'm so passionate about sharing my story is so that others can share their gifts and live their dreams. It was a blessing passed onto me; therefore I'm passing it on to you. When my husband died, he left two gifts: his first gift was the ability for me to step into who I am to live in my purpose; his second gift was giving me to the world to be able to share these gifts. A great book that also touched on this topic with a scenario quite similar to mine is *The Gift Giver* by Jennifer Hawkins. Jennifer also became a widow with two kids, and her husband also passed on to leave her with a gift.

Ask yourself what fuels your spirit; those are your dreams and passion for fulfillment toward your purpose. When they are left ignored, we oftentimes seek distractions or disruptive outlets trying to fill that void. To clarify, notice the word "passion." Don't mistake the word "passion" with all joyful feelings of things you like to do. When people hear the words "dreams" and "passion," they have the misconception that they are fantasy words that come with no sacrifice, challenges, or even pain. The root definition of "passion" is to sacrifice, such as Passion of Christ. Pursuing your calling and dreams will come with sacrifices and pain, so passion and desire are needed that will enable you to overcome the difficulties.

One of the challenges that I faced as a single mom when building my own businesses was the complexity of managing the role as a mother and aligning it with my responsibilities as the owner of a business. As most entrepreneurs, when you first get started, we wear all the hats of operation until we're able to leverage or hire assistance; capitalize on your strengths and hire your weakness. I was by far not perfect in every aspect in the business world, so I had to learn and develop some skill sets.

As a single mom I had to learn how to navigate through challenges. Later I learned that these challenges were really opportunities in disguise. There were a couple business events where I had to bring my two children along with me. Now, can you imagine going to a weeklong event not only to learn about business practices but also to network and then having to volunteer to staff it? Luckily there was a children's program during the day that kept my kids occupied, but since I was a volunteer staff, that meant long hours—getting up early and ending late at night. A couple nights throughout the week, the kids had to sit in the back of the room. At another event I attended with them, I started to have this mommy guilt creep over me. I would say it was coming from that little voice we all have that just breeds negativity; therefore, I chose not to feed it.

Even though the kids sat in the back of the room at this event, they were in a positive environment, listening to everyone's story of how they overcame adversity to be the success that they are today. Can you imagine if you were eight and nine years old hearing, seeing, and personally meeting people such as Ron Klein, who automated Wall Street and created the credit card strip and the MLS; Frank Shankwitz, founder of Make-A-Wish Foundation; Sharon Lechter, the former CEO of Rich Dad Poor Dad and best-selling author; Bob Proctor, the legendary motivational speaker; Berny Dohrmann, the founder of CEO Space International, who shared his learnings from Napoleon Hill (and now my children call Mr. Dohrmann "Uncle"); Sherita Herring, a coach who has helped individuals from various industries raise millions of dollars; Erin Saxton, who was the former producer of *The View* and who shared her pearls of wisdom from her own mentor Barbara Walters over dinner; and one of my favorites, Dr. Gladys McGarey, the Mother of Holistic Medicine. These aren't your typical "events" where we sit and listen to speeches all day or where everyone is there to hand out business cards promoting themselves. I've been able to develop authentic relationships with phenomenal individuals. At the end of the day, whatever your definition of success is, whatever product or service you are promoting, we are all in the people business first.

Meeting these individuals has been a privilege and a blessing, but I don't get caught up with a person's title or list of accomplishments because I have met people who are just as talented, who have beautiful spirits, who share their gifts, but who may not be recognized to the public eye. You need to develop relationships first, then business, even if it means that the relationship may not directly benefit you. Let me give you an example—you may want to highlight this section.

You reap what you sow. There's nothing new under the sun. I'm sure you've read that part in the Bible already. When you meet people, do not have the selfish intention of meeting or interacting with them only for your benefit. This is how I've been able to become successful and blessed beyond measures without even knowing it.

I'll use one example to keep it simple. I was introduced to a man named Peter. Eventually, as Peter and I developed a rapport, I introduced him to my business. Whether he was interested in my business or not, I trusted Peter enough and respected his work that I actually acted as a "connector" for one of my friends—I'll call him Luke. Peter ended up helping Luke's son with a pretty serious illness. Now, what would have happened if I decided to discard the introduction to Peter because I had selfish intentions and wanted to connect with him only if he was interested in my business? The connection to Luke would have never happened.

God does work through people, and we are all here to serve, even in the "smallest" way (from our vantage point) like making an introduction. When you're able to develop relationships with people and build trust, it increases your influence. People are going to naturally gravitate toward you; therefore, your business grows, and you reap what you sow.

In the Love and Relationship section I brought up Gary Chapman's work on the 5 Love Languages. The same concept applies here in success and happiness. There are tons of personality profile models or EQ (Emotional Intelligence) tests out there, including Briggs Myers, Enneagram, Hermann Brain Dominance, GEMS, etc., that will allow you to use a baseline to know your strengths and others' strengths to best serve your career, relationships, and more.

I took a couple of these tests myself. I encourage you to take a simple one. I remember looking at one, and it was just way too confusing. Another was actually great, but I needed an expert to interpret my results. Although the results were accurate in defining who I was and how I interacted with people, it still left me with the challenge of how do I interact with other people? How do I know which personality type they are and what motivates them? How do I speak their language?

The point is, whatever business you're in, whether you work for someone or have your own product or service, we're all in the people business. If you're a parent, you're still in the people business communicating with your kids. Why not invest time in understanding people, how they think, and how they make decisions? It's about communicating to them, not taking a test that already tells us who we are. (I hope you at least know yourself.)

You were born to be divinely successful and to live happily. God didn't give us a purpose to be miserable. Granted, we may have to be in jobs or roles temporarily to meet our needs and responsibilities, refine our skills, etc., but don't exhaust your time, effort, energy, and finances if it doesn't align with your priorities, purpose, and passion.

Going for our dreams takes courage. It may seem intimidating at first, but know that you are not alone. I recall talking to a friend, Joy, one day, and she was telling me a childhood story of how her friends were teasing and daring her to dive off a diving board. As scared as she was, and even though the dive was not perfect, she did it while others couldn't overcome their own fears to do the same. The point of the story is that even though she belly flopped, she conquered her fear—even with imperfections. It is only then that we learn how to swim and thrive; otherwise, we are inhibited, surrender to fear, and get stuck in survival mode.

Exercising faith takes practice, but once you experience its manifestations, you'll follow it more freely with flow. About a year after I left my corporate career, I made another move—I literally moved. My two kids and I moved from Northern California to Southern California. I had no close friends or close relatives in the vicinity. The closest relative was a cousin in another city about forty-five miles away and long-lost relatives about sixty miles in the other direction. I did have business associates north and south of me, but basically I had to establish new footing.

Everyone from my family, friends, and business contacts inquired as to why I made this drastic move. My reply was, "Why not? The weather is great. We'll be close to the ocean. I work from home anyway. Joy's G.I.F.T. (nonprofit) can be anywhere. I can start a new life. I've always had a desire to move to Southern California." But above all those reasons, which not everyone will grasp, is that my faith guided my flow to move where I ended up. Let's just say for simplicity that I had divine guidance surrounding me to guide me and protect me. Only a couple people know the details of the "serendipitous" (I put that word in quotes because I don't believe in luck or chance) occurrences that unfolded that allowed me to move 500 miles away with ease. And as I continued to allow faith to flow, everything else continued to unfold and come together as the kids and I settled into our new place.

I sit here now, writing this book before it even becomes a bestseller, in the most perfect and magical place a writer can be: the view of the fifth fairway of the golf course, a short drive along the coast to the beautiful blue ocean and warm sand beaches. I love watching God's work as I pick up the puzzle pieces and connect the dots as to how everything comes together and how he enables me with resources and connections to make my dreams come true, the dreams I have dedicated to serving others.

Don't read my story and be misled by faith alone. You must sail with action and not just stand or plan on the shoreline. "*Faith without works is dead*"(James 2:14-26). Live your dream; don't just stand behind it to follow it. It doesn't have to be implemented perfectly or done all at once, but it's what we're all here for, to live the one life we are given. You can choose the dream or the nightmare. I'm living my dream, with mistakes and all and lessons learned.

So how do you define your happiness and success? First, you must understand the concept that success and happiness is an equation, not a formula[See example as you read on]. Also understand that this is YOUR equation. Don't define the elements/variables in the equation by comparing yourself to others or by what your friends and family say you should be doing. Everyone's threshold and indicators for success and happiness are respectfully unique. Some may say that I was crazy to sell my beautiful 3,500-square-foot home on a quarter acre on top of the hill with a phenomenal million-dollar view to downsize to a smaller place 500 miles away. But I was redefining what was important to me and what my happy and success equation looked like. Do assess what's important to you and your family, your responsibilities, your goals and passions. Do calculate the risk, but don't spend too much time calculating and not actually moving forward implementing!

There's no such thing as getting ready to get ready—just keep moving. Don't feel like you have to make such drastic and radical changes to start. Take the teardrop approach if that's more suitable for your situation. The teardrop method is planning and doing something toward your purpose and passion, even if it's setting up a couple meetings per week collaborating with a new network of potential clients, customers, business partners, etc., or maybe it's attending personal development seminars, networking mixers, learning a new skill, etc.

Two equation enhancers are mentors and the power of leverage. To collapse timeframes toward your success, learn from someone who already paved the way. Seek the appropriate coach/mentor; you wouldn't hire a fitness coach to create a workout plan for you if you were seeking financial planning, would you? Learn from their mistakes and their shortcuts.

Now, one thing I always want to highlight is that just because they have results, doesn't mean they're the right leader for you to follow. For example, if you wanted to earn $100,000 per month, would you compromise your values to be mentored by someone in a drug cartel, or would you sell your soul toward evil and immoral business deals? Also, you may want to assess what they had to compromise or sacrifice to get those results. Did their path look realistic, acceptable, and adaptable for you? Did their success come with a price of a marriage that ended with a divorce, and if so, is this the same path you're willing to take? Or do their kids resent them because they are never home or involved with their school activities? Basically, what price did they have to pay to get where they are?

The other enhancer is leverage, which can come in various forms: leveraging established affiliations or collaborations with other like-minded individuals; leveraging your existing talents and skills; leveraging the relationships you currently have with various people; even leveraging a business opportunity as a vehicle or platform to catapult your own endeavors.

For example, when I first left the corporate world to transition from an engineer to an entrepreneur, I leveraged the industry of network marketing to enable me to continue my writing as an author and philanthropy in founding my nonprofit, empowering women and youth. In my opinion, there's a population that carries a negative connotation of this industry because there's an element of that "white elephant" that is not openly addressed. People would be more respectful of and receptive to the industry if all the truth about the intricacies of the industry were addressed. No industry is perfect—network marketing, the corporate world, nonprofit enterprises, etc. From personal experience, the industry is very rewarding in many facets: monetarily, spiritually, business, and personal development, and it's simply gratifying when you help other people with passion, truth, and integrity.

Being in network marketing wasn't my end purpose, but it served as a vehicle that allowed me to sharpen my people skills (I was an introverted person having sat in a cubicle in the corporate world for fourteen years), grow my business acumen, work on my personal development, network with people from various industries, and position myself to help others. To give you a visualization, I "drove" this vehicle. My vision (my ultimate goal-purpose) was on the dashboard, my passion was the one driving the vehicle, and the product-opportunity was the means/money adding to the gas tank for the vehicle. That's not to say this is a vehicle for everyone, but I just want to encourage you to explore outside your box of comfort. This is the only way you'll grow.

The skills I learned in network marketing are transferable in any business, and the relationships I've developed with people— whether they joined my business or not—are priceless. To this day, my heart is touched when I randomly get an e-mail or text message from a prospect that just wanted to reach out to me to say thank you for inspiring them with the opportunity I presented. Even though the business may not have been for them, they were inspired and impacted. My memory and heart will always be imprinted with what transpired as a result of just developing a rapport with them. If I don't earn another dime from my network marketing business again, I can at least say I've learned how to connect with people. I can at least pass on a smile to them or a spark of inspiration and maybe even guidance for their own path.

I've always been nice and friendly to people in general, but putting forth an extra effort makes a difference. I remember leaving a luncheon one afternoon, and I was carpooling with a friend. As we were leaving the parking structure, I was paying the attendant the fee and said, "Thank you, [name]," and my friend gave me this look as if he was shocked that I knew that person's name. I replied, "What? Their name was on the window booth." He said he was just surprised because nobody does that. Really, are we too busy or caught up in our own worlds that we have lost our basic humanity to acknowledge another person by their first name or just say thank you?!

Going back to the topic of business. When you are faced with having to make a business decision, it is up to you as the individual to take the responsibility for making that decision. It is not just when the outcome of that decision goes correctly and according to plan and things are great, but it also means taking ownership when the outcome isn't as expected. We cannot blame others or be angry at the world if the outcome wasn't necessarily what we anticipated.

When making a decision, try to assess the entire situation before coming to an assumed conclusion. Once you make that decision, own it and don't waver between the two; then you'll see the true manifestation of your destiny. Wavering and wondering has cost me delays, frustration, stress, monetary loss, and chaos.

When it comes to your dreams/goals or supporting someone else's, you should believe in it firmly—not contingent upon anyone else's approval. There will be those who support you and those who do not. You have to choose not to allow the non-supporters to hinder you from continuing what you truly believe in.

"We are all called to do something different but we are all born with the same grace, gratitude, love, and joy to do it."

There will come a time when it's your turn to be called to fulfill your purpose, and you will be tested. Family and friends may not believe or support you because they don't see your same vision, and that's okay. It will be obvious who they are once you hit a milestone (to them), such as being on the Oprah show, giving them money, or maybe they're using a product you invented or they see your face on a magazine or movie. THEN they'll rally to support you and tell all their friends that you go waaayyy back. Really? Did they really have your back?! This is where forgiveness comes in with grace, gratitude, love, and joy. Keep sharing and spreading your joys with the blessings of a smile.

For those that have a spiritual belief that may or may not have experienced this yet, it is outlined in the *Dream Giver* book that we are tested to give up our dreams for a bigger one for God's ultimate glory for the greater good, not just ours. I will share a little here on how this is true with my own experiences. In Jeremiah 29:4-7, the Bible refers to how we are to bloom or prosper where we are planted.

We may plant the seeds of our success and wealth, but it is God that creates the increase and growth. Where we prosper in our success and dreams is interwoven with our relationship with God. When the nation of Israel was exiled to Babylon, their instructions were to blossom where they were now planted. To me, that sounds like adversity. When adversity comes our way, do we seek to strengthen our relationship, and trust and surrender to God? Do we see the blessing in each adversity so that we can prosper, or are we tainted with negativity?

With my particular stories, it was a glorious dream of mine since middle school or high school to work for Intel. While I was in high school, I remember listening to a guest speaker who was an engineer at Intel. I approached her after her speech, and she ended up giving me her business card. I would envision my own name with Intel's e-mail domain, as if I had an e-mail address with them. I think there's a saying for that one: "thoughts are things." It was my dream to work there, and yes, I got that dream. I spent years there, grateful for the opportunity, until one day that same inner knowing that gave me the dream to work there was calling me again. It was calling me for a different dream.

In the *Dream Giver* book, the character Ordinary was finally building his dream in the City of Anybodies until one day the Dream Giver himself called upon him to let him know that his plans of a bigger dream lay outside the city walls that he was currently building. It was validating to know when I read this that I was not alone. I even believe that sometimes we are to complete a certain task or season of tasks to lead us to our destiny. For my particular example, when I left the corporate world, I was working on developing a software app. Now that I look at that dream, it lead me to where I am today, building and living my dreams as if the initial one was my own "carrot" to get me here.

When pursuing your dreams, you'll probably grow through a difficult transition as you try to navigate the path. You may feel as if you are trying to do everything possible, but certain obstacles are setting you back. I don't think those circumstances are really "setbacks." I think those circumstances (which could be finances, relationships, or other things that get in the way)are developing your character as you grow and continue to shine as you learn from them, if you allow it.

I think what I've learned from all my adversities is that in the moment it does feel overwhelming, but there's always a benefit to going through it (Napoleon Hill)—again, if you allow yourself to accept it. It's like the alchemy of adversity. Sometimes when we "go against the grain," it is a true test to strengthen and develop us. However, sometimes if you really listen to your inner-being or speak to God himself, you'll know that oftentimes there is too much resistance in a path that you're not even supposed to be on.

Through it all, in discovering your path and defining your own success and happiness, you will find peace once you realize where you can be happy and flourish, and others around you can experience the true beauty and gifts within you.

One of my gifts is being able to inspire people to bring out their own gifts to share and to provide healing, no matter what the adversity. My other gift came from my share of challenges. I've learned how to find the gold in adversity. When you stay true to the fundamentals of how we were created (with love) and why we were created (to live joy), you are strengthened when adversity arises and you'll be better equipped to rise above it.

This does not make anyone immune though. As Napoleon Hill stated, "Every adversity has within it the seed of an equivalent or greater benefit." The key word is "seed." Do not expect a flower to fully blossom out of the rubble you just went through. The seed must be nurtured and nourished by choice; then it begins to grow and blossom. Guess what this seed produces…your hidden gems of gifts. Utilize these gifts to experience joy. We should be appreciating everyone's gifts, joys, and blessings and uniting as a whole as opposed to always dividing and segregating ourselves based on the ways we're different and better than the other person.

Defining success and happiness is dynamic for everyone. Everyone has their own definition to begin with, as well as different phases in our lives that influence how we define them. Happiness is an acquirement of an emotion; the secret to everlasting fulfillment is joy. Joy is a constant emotional state, compared to happiness that can change depending on how we define it. Joy is purely within each of our hearts since it is a gift from our Creator.

"Stop hitting the snooze button and wake up to your dreams and live it!"

"Why have you given up on your dreams when the one who created you and gave you those dreams has never given up on you?"

How do you define success and happiness? If you were to paint a picture, what would it look like? With the colors of joy, you need to paint not only the next chapter in your life but the next level. Would it be a dream career you've always wanted? Would it be starting your own business? Maybe it's finding your soul mate? Are kids in this picture? Where would you travel? How much money do you see yourself having? How much money would you give? What would you buy? Does your picture look like it could be related to your purpose in life? What emotions are you experiencing? What does it feel like? Do you feel excited, fulfilled and whole, anxious, happy, secure, obedient, powerful, limitless, grateful, joyful?

The picture you just painted on your canvas shows how you have attached the emotions you want to acquire based on the manifestations of what's in the picture.

Does your picture have a meaning or was it all about proving something? What meaning have you attached to your picture of success and happiness? We all set benchmarks for ourselves, but who is it all for and why is it for them? Is it our ego that measures our success and happiness by everything we pictured? Is the picture and what it looks like conditioned by society and even our family and friends?

When it was time to reassess all those questions for myself with my business-life coach and financial planners, we noted everything on my list for my life vision and my mission statements. Having certain items and accomplishing certain task wasn't just about obtaining the benchmark. It was directionally proportionate to my purpose—what I valued and believed in.

Note that I said this was with a "life coach" and that we discussed my vision and my mission statements for "my life." Why is it that some people have a coach only for fitness or business? And why is it that people have mission and vision statements for their business but not their own life? If they don't own a business, they probably memorized and honor their employer's mission and vision statements, so why not create one for themselves? We plan our vacations and our holidays, so don't our lives deserve the same honor and attention?

Oftentimes we prove our success and happiness to ourselves and others in the form of acquisition. I'm guilty of it just as you are. We buy cars, homes, and other materialistic items simply just to acquire them, consciously or subconsciously. This doesn't mean we are not allowed to spend our money and acquire nice items in life, but I challenge you to question why you are doing it. Is it related to having a meaning to your purpose in life, or is it just the ego? At least be honest and acknowledge it. An ego in check can be a healthy one versus one that's in denial. Here are a couple of my items that were in my life vision and mission statements.

- Having a jet – this meant two things: one would be acquiring the benchmark for my kids since it is something they envision as success. The other would serve as a purpose toward my own life purpose. Having the jet meant my businesses has grown enough to financially allow me to purchase the jet and to be able to serve other countries with the ease of accessibility. This means my capacity and vessel to give has increased.

- Having two different homes – one home would be like my previous dream home but on a larger scale, and the other home would be quainter and on a remote, private island. A little bit of my ego still wants the big home, but it would mainly serve to help others believe in success and happiness. Sometimes we need to allow others to borrow our belief and success to help build their own.

You see, we as a society have conditioned our minds to have a certain status quo regarding what success should look like. I remember listening to Rita Davenport (award-winning speaker and author) at a conference a couple times, and she said to the crowd, "Do you know why I wear two watches? One of them is a cheap Timex but I can see the numbers on here, and the other is a $35,000 Rolex that YOU can see!" So, what if you didn't know Rita as she sat in your local coffee shop at the table next to you without all her jewelry? Would you perceive her as successful? Or, if she was wearing it, would that blinding Rolex catch your attention and since you've been conditioned to equate expensive items with success, have you now categorized her as successful?

The other home of mine would be quainter on a remote island with privacy to allow myself to re-center and rebalance with no distractions to the ego.

In one of Dani Johnson's audios, she said and I'll paraphrase, *"You have to be set free from chasing cash before you can be trusted with the influence of people."*

You can only get so far with your success if all you chase after is the money; it's the people that come first. Do people sense that you really care about them and that you're providing something they actually want or need, or are you only after their money?

I've made good choices and choices that weren't so good when it came to finances, but God sees where our hearts are. When you are given a blessing—in this particular case in finances—ask yourself two questions;

(1) Did I really deserve to have this money because I earned it?

The second question is most important:

(2) Do I deserve to keep it?

There are spiritual laws that govern success and wealth. We have to be good stewards of our blessings.

(Matthew 25:14 Parable of the Bags of Gold)

With my story in *Chase The Challenge and Conquer*, I shared the foolish spending my late husband and I did that wasted money. Both of us made a decent income at Intel, yet we not only built a home, but we also added more upgrades to the new home on top of credit card bills, student loans, and car payments—oh, and we had kids' expenses! Finances can put a toll on a marriage.

I'm grateful my ego wasn't as big as our debt because I actually listened to my late husband when we had to make some adjustments in our lifestyle. We sold our home to downsize and rent. (You can picture the emotional wreck I was when we were having this conversation about having to sell our home that we just built.) We moved closer to work; we budgeted our spending; we paid down bills.

When my husband passed away, our household income went from dual incomes to just mine. Before I continue with the finance pieces, I want women to recall the statement I made about putting *you* back on your to-do list. This means putting you on the plan to make sure you are also taken cared of along with everyone else you attend to. Can you imagine if, as a widow, I now had to gain skills to be valuable in a competitive marketplace and seek work to provide for the household? I'm grateful that I was in a position to bring in income for my family. So, going back to being good stewards of our blessings and finances … I've made some good choices and some choices that weren't so good with the life insurance that I did receive from my husband.

The first thing I did was pay off all the debt: credit cards, student loans, etc. I think I had only one car payment, and I was even getting heartburn about getting a car because I didn't want any payments. I did get a new car only because the one I had kept breaking down, and I didn't feel safe with a broken car and two small kids. So, I say that those at least were good choices. I also paid a family member's mortgage off.

The not-so-good choice was the timing of building a home. And I say "not so good" because I did receive some happiness and fulfillment out of it, but had I been wiser, I could have saved myself some difficult predicaments. I didn't build just an ordinary home; it was a custom home. A major lesson I learned was not to make such a drastic and large decision while in an emotional state.

I want you to try and picture yourself in this beautiful, 3,500-square-foot home with a stone turret entry that sat on top of a hill on a quarter acre with a view that could see the city skyline twenty-five miles away. Every color at sunset beamed through the windows of every part of the house. The morning sunrise from the master bedroom balcony often had views of hot air balloons. The master bathroom didn't need a TV because the bay windows by the tub had a view of the stars above. A yoga platform in the backyard felt like a peaceful setting of a retreat next to the waterfall. And then there's this voice you hear that says, *"It's time. It's time to move. Will you trust to trade one dream for another?"*

I ended up renting my home and moved two miles away to a smaller home to rent in a neighborhood that my late husband used to live in—like literally on the same street. It was funny how that worked, out of all the places I found and that it was available. But you see, I wasn't completely obedient to God's request when I heard that question being asked of me. It wasn't like I was "punished," but it just delayed things and made it a little more difficult for me, not to mention it cost me time and money to move twice.

I've always known in my heart that I would be moving to Southern California, but during this time, I was willing to invest in the relationship that I was in, instead of my calling. Well, living at this rental lasted only nine months. When I committed to finally moving to Southern California, it was as if the floodgates of blessings flowed magically—actually, it felt like the gates were taken completely off the hinges. I'm so appreciative that others around me witnessed these flow of blessings because it strengthen them. My home sold for the price I asked for in less than a month, and I didn't even have to put it on the market! The rental I was leasing was a twelve-month contract, meaning I would have to find a replacement tenant or pay the continued rent. The rental market there was pretty competitive, and at one point we had a tenant lined up to take over my lease but they backed out. This caused a delay of only a couple days, but looking back on it now, it was the right timing for the right tenants to take over my lease. Had the first one gone through, I wouldn't be where I am today. I would have chosen the adjacent city, which I had always known within me that the area was just supposed to be my "off the grid fun area," not my sanctuary for home and peace.

During this time, I fully trusted in God, even during the moments of uncertainty between the gaps of time when my house was in escrow, when I was applying for a rental for a new place, and when I was finding a new tenant. It was like having a game of which comes first, the chicken or the egg? Do I secure a new place to live first or wait for a new tenant? Of course, the most logical answer would be find a tenant first, but that would mean I could possibly compromise on a place I really didn't like for the sake of time of having to move out. Keep in mind I was relocating 500 miles away, so it wasn't like I could just store my items at a storage center and sleep at a friend's house for a couple days.

This is just a small portion of the "serendipitous" occurrences of the "how" that led me here to Southern California. God continues to bless my kids' and my paths as he continues to reveal the "why" I am here. He sees that I made good choices and not-so-good choices regarding the financial blessings I was granted.

Something to note: when you spend money and time to

grow yourself personally and spiritually, it is also an investment, and not just in business. I do see the fruition of the seeds I planted because they have increased my influence. The governance of which I'm responsible for is a direct outcome of those blessings. When I speak on influence, it is not about influencing people to serve you; it is about you serving them first with humility and humanity.

"It's the invisible that creates the visible, the roots create the results of the fruit" T. HarvEcker

From the 4 R's Program –Happiness & Success Equation

You can find your equation for happiness, success, and prosperity. And yes, it is an equation and not a formula. I'm using the math terminology of equations vs. formula loosely here since one can argue that a formula is an equation. But what I'm trying to convey is that a formula is restricted and defined by its variables.

Let's look at Newton's formula for force: $F = ma$. To find force, multiply the mass of an object by its acceleration. $F = ma$, notice "m" and "a" are the only variables. When comparing an equation to a formula, there can be other variables:

$$a + b = d \ or \ (a + b) + c = d.$$

So how do these equations apply to happiness and success? Everyone has their own equation with various variables. One can add or subtract variables that would most likely equate to happiness and success. The following are just a few examples of these variables with which you are now familiar:

Mind - Meditate and pray, have a connection with our Creator, control our own minds, set goals, study

Body - Eat consciously healthy, exercise, rest, recover, cleanse

Soul - Meditate to be able to connect within, align with your passion

These are just a few examples of the variables in one's equation. Your equation will differ from someone else's. Equations for happiness and success are never set like a formula because the variables change as our life progresses and evolves, so even our own equations will change.

For example, what if your definition of success looked like this equation:

$$x + y + z = Success$$

x = obtaining a PhD, y = getting married,

z = getting dream home

Now what would happen if life threw you a curve ball and your "z" variable of getting your dream home was foreclosed? Well, now I'm sure that "z" is out of that equation. Do you have a different outlook now on just $x+y$ = Success, or are you still trying to add or replace the "z = dream home"? My point is that no two equations for people are ever the same; even your own equation will change as your life goes through stages.

Even further, what if two people had the same definition of success and their equations had identical variable definitions? Even then the variables themselves can vary; one person can spend eight years in school while the other took ten years to obtain their PhD.

For those that don't love math, let's look at another analogy. Say that you hired a trainer to help you lose weight. The trainer gives you all these variables to equal weight loss: do this amount of cardio time; this amount of weights; eat this, not that; and on and on.... Wouldn't we all agree that these variable definitions are just guidelines? One must modify the program specifically for their own variables because like that saying goes, "No two snowflakes are alike." Someone may need only forty minutes of cardio to see results while the other person needs sixty minutes, yet cardio still $= x$ in both equations.

In order to be happy and successful, you must first ask yourself what makes you happy and what your definition of success is.

To have optimal results, calibrate your equation. You have to identify which areas are in deficit versus a surplus.

Ricochet Back at Life

A quote in *Chase The Challenge and Conquer* reads, "Sometimes life deals you a tough hand but the only way to win is to play it." Another one says, "Life can throw you a curveball," but this one just leaves you dangling. My thought is, if you're not ready to catch that curveball, move out of the way until you're ready to **ricochet back**.

Don't fall on the field as a victim forever. You have the option of getting back up. If anyone can do it, YOU can because I have.

What curveball caught you off guard? Did you have to

downgrade your lifestyle due to the economic downturn? Are you a victim of a tragedy or crime? Are you maybe overwhelmed with all your fame and fortune? We can't predict what will come our way, but we can somewhat predict how we are going to react. Based on how well we think we know ourselves, we can prepare ourselves with the necessary tools in life to overcome just about anything.

Think about how you react to any stressful situation now. How do you handle it? Do you have to make a conscious effort to stay calm and just breathe, or did your blood pressure just skyrocket out of control? How do you react when things don't go as planned? Are you the type to panic in a whirlwind, or are you able to control your emotions and formulate a Plan B? Everyone has a different personality, and what works for me may or may not work for the next person. It's like success: there's no formula for success, but there are definitely elements in everyone's specific equation that aid in a positive outcome. These elements make up a strong foundation—a foundation built on faith, a support network, knowing your strengths and weakness, being consistent, believing in yourself, being healthy, creating and integrating positive habits into your daily lifestyle, and creating a balance among your mind, body, and soul.

Where people fall short is when they realize that you can't just rely on amplifying your strengths to ricochet back at life. How do you know if those are the tools you need when you're presented with an obstacle in life? Sometimes we don't need a sledgehammer to get the job done; a regular pocket hammer will do. My point is, be consistent with improving your weak points as you are polishing your strengths. That's how you become stronger overall as a person. I can't remember which track-and-field athlete was interviewed after winning an event recently at the London Olympics, but I remember him saying that he was able to accomplish winning because he trained on improving his weak areas. This provided a balance that made him a stronger athlete and better competitor.

All of us have a toolbox for life, already equipped with the right tools, but we need to know what's inside the box in order to polish them and know which ones we need to use at any given moment. So the next time life deals you a tough hand or throws you a curveball, RICOCHET BACK!

The Power of BELIEVING

Our mind is a powerful tool as it is. Amplify it to align with your body and soul to create YOU.

> *BELIEVE in our Creator.*

> *BELIEVE in others, but most importantly,*

> *BELIEVE in yourself.*

> *BELIEVE you are given the strength.*

> *BELIEVE you are given the confidence.*

> *BELIEVE you are given the knowledge.*

> *BELIEVE you are given the choice.*

All you have to do is claim what's already given to you!

Ask anyone who is happy, healthy, healed, and successful if they believed in their own goals, their strengths, and their own choices. I guarantee you the answer will be yes.

Once our mind is determined to believe, our body will

follow. However, one must be spiritually intune in order to know what our soul's passion is so that we can know the true aspect of what to believe. You can't just program the mind to "believe" in something if the soul's passion doesn't align. It may work temporarily, but soon enough conflict and an unsettled feeling will arise and cause destruction. You have to believe and feel. And when I say "feel," it's not an emotional feeling invoked by our minds; the feeling is rooted deep in our soul's passion.

"My faith is greater than my fear."

REBALANCE YOUR RELATIONSHIPS

CHAPTER 5

Parenting

———————— ≈ ————————

Parenting is a lifelong career itself. However, there is no manual, there's no job description, there is no pay structure, and there's no clocking in or out. It's lifelong, on-the-job training. As I mentioned in the beginning chapters, the title "mom" by itself has many sub-roles.

There may be resources, support groups, and books out there on parenting, but we all know there's no one glove that fits all—not even this section you're now reading.

A Pew Research survey found that about half (53 percent) of all working parents with children under age eighteen say it is difficult for them to balance the responsibilities of their job with the responsibilities of their family. Pew Research also indicates that roughly 60 percent of two-parent households with children have both parents working.

(http://www.pewsocialtrends.org/2013/03/14/modern-parenthood-roles-of-moms-and-dads-converge-as-they-balance-work-and-family/)

With both parents working, we should be aware of what is being compromised and/or impacted on the child's end: time spent with their parents, their schoolwork, their behavior, and their health. Imagine a household where both parents work and the kids have school and sports activities. Do you think it's uncommon for dinner to be served through the drive-thru or pizza delivery? Are we being the role models we want for our young generation?

Now, I'm not ridiculing the parents who both have to work because frankly that was my household when I was married. I just encourage you to bring awareness to your circumstance and make the necessary adjustments to address what's important for you.

My late husband and I had to make adjustments for our family. For example, we chose to sell our home to be closer to work so that we didn't spend so much time commuting to work with two babies. We downsized to a smaller home to have a more comfortable lifestyle, and we also worked together when it came to household duties and caring for the children. For example, instead of buying take-out for dinner after work, I went home to cook a healthy meal while he picked up the kids from daycare, and then he kept the kids occupied while I was in the kitchen.

Simple adjustments like these are key elements to a harmonious and healthy home. Parenting doesn't just mean rearing children; it means working with the person with whom you had the child as a team (no matter if you are still together or not).

Another element that goes unnoticed when we become

parents is how it affects the union of the marriage or relationship. There was some sort of intimacy in the relationship (hence the formation of the kids), but what happens once we become parents?

I will put myself on the hot seat and speak for myself. When I became a mom, it was as if I forgot to be me and forgot to be a wife. It was ALL about the kids first. It's a wonderful role to be a mother, but it's still imperative to maintain our own identities and to continue to foster our other relationship/marriage—that strengthens the foundation for the union of the family as a whole. This is a natural flow of order. When I speak about "order," I refer to how love flows through the hierarchies of everyone's role in the family. When parents love on each other, it is passed on to the kids. When this natural flow is broken, when one parent is passing all their love to the child only, the children are not positioned in the hierarchy to necessary give back "up the stream" to the parents or the parent lacking the received flow.

Family time is as important as adult time. With the daily demands from our multiple roles, sometimes by the end of the day, we have no energy or love to pour into our companions. The smallest adjustments and effort will have long-lasting impacts: making an effort daily to just connect and have a conversation about each other's day, reaffirming to the other person the value they bring into your life, complimenting the other person, or even (on a weekly and monthly basis) setting aside a date night for adult time only. On date night you can be grown-ups again and not have to worry about being a parent.

Now let's discuss the controversial topic of multitasking. Again, as women we have many roles, and we have a unique ability to perform all of them. However, all these roles come with a set of demands, and even though technology enables us to become more efficient, it doesn't always translate to being effective.

Have you seen those pictures with a mother holding a baby in one hand while she's talking on the phone, typing on her laptop with the other hand, has food cooking in the background on the stove? Well, everything technically gets done: food is on the table, the baby is cared for, the e-mail was sent out, and the phone call was resolved. However, it's no wonder that women are so physically, mentally, and emotionally drained and overwhelmed.

A *Forbes* article, "How Multi-tasking Hurts Your Brain",

http://www.forbes.com/sites/work-in-progress/2013/01/15/how-multitasking-hurts-your-brain-and-your-effectiveness-at-work/, highlighted scientific studies that have shown that the brain cannot effectively and efficiently switch between tasks; therefore, when multitasking, time is wasted and productivity results are negatively affected. Going back to the earlier pictorial of the multitasking mother, yes, she was able to complete the task, but consider how it was completed and what was compromised for to accomplish it.

While I was still an engineer working in the corporate world, I remember having to rush to give my baby daughter a quick bath before bedtime. Then I would lock myself in the master closet (the only quiet place in the house) in case she got fussy and didn't want to fall asleep. I would close myself up in there with my laptop so that I could call into a meeting that was taking place in another time zone. Looking back at it now, I did what I had to do, but those habits were not sustainable.

Multitasking has its effects:

- Excessive stimulation preventing sleep
- Decreased productivity
- Lack of focus (having to recreate your thought pattern)
  - Stress

A 2009 study by Clifford Nass, PhD, and others at Stanford University shows that participants who multitask the most are distracted by unimportant information that is stored in their short-term memory

(http://smallbusiness.chron.com/bad-effects-multitasking-32419.html).

Here are some practices that can help become more productive:

- Go on a digital diet
- Plan and schedule
- Be in your mode

Go on a digital diet! I learned this in one of the radio interviews I did with Berny Dohrmann (founder of the largest and most recognized business growth conferences – CEO Space International). What does going on a digital diet look like? Schedule times when you are going to be on and off your e-mail accounts, social media accounts, texting, taking phone calls, etc. For example, set apart certain times during your day when you're not checking your multiple social media accounts; you can then graduate to doing a longer periods of your digital diet. Now, if your business depends on your online presence, schedule auto-updates or have someone be your social media person for a few days.

As a society we've become addicted to and are

bombarded by technology because of our dependency on it and the ease of access to it. This is even a process of practice for me. As I'm writing this book and this particular section, I not only turned off my e-mails and phone, but I also went next door to the country club because there is no cell coverage there. I too can fall into the distraction trap. Before you know it, one e-mail or one phone call or one text message here or there can become thirty lost minutes, and I have to switch my focus to get back on track. Planning your day with a schedule minimizes unnecessary distractions.

When I have my mommy hat on, I make an effort to stay in mommy-mode. This is not the time for me to be an engineer and debug a technical issue over the phone or be an author and in my writing zone. How fair would it be to your employer if you were at your workplace in mommy-mode, planning your son's birthday, or on your personal social media accounts? Don't our kids deserve the same attention and respect?

Notice I said that it's a process for me to practice and that it takes effort; nobody is perfect. Granted, there are certain situations you have to accomplish with multitasking, but these should be short-term sacrifices.

It's imperative that you sit down with your family to manage expectations. Maybe there are certain school events that you cannot attend because they conflict with your work travel, or maybe you can physically be at your child's sporting event but mentally your attention is a little diverted by the work that's on the laptop that you brought because of a project deadline.

When we become parents, whatever happens to our fun and joy factors? As parents we can still be the authoritative figures and caregivers to our children, but wouldn't it make the experience better for everyone if it were fun and pleasant? Laugh, play, interact, and communicate with your children. This can be difficult because our attention is often diverted with distractions. Even I have to practice this. When we have family game night in my home, I have to practice not looking at my phone, checking e-mails, texting, or doing a grocery list in my head. Being present with your child as a parent takes practice, but it brings such indescribable rewards, and it imprints on your child's memory in ways that are priceless. It's also very effective in that when it's time for you to focus on other things like work, you will have spent time with your kids and you won't feel guilty about working.

Parenting can be fun and creative while being effective as well. Kids are creative and love to dream. Why not make a vision board with them and let them decide what pictures to create? This exercise—the power of visualization, goal setting, having a positive mental attitude, and teamwork—is simple and fun yet extremely powerful to instill at a young age. What child likes to do chores? Well, what if you made the process of completing the chores a fun routine? Blast their favorite music. Create a reward chart with them. Have them set a goal that once they accomplish so many chores they earn something they value. Have the kids in the kitchen cooking and baking with you. There are many ways to make it fun.

These simple examples serve multiple purposes. When kids engage with the cooking, you are not only teaching them with life skills, they are also learning healthy eating habits. They are more interested in eating what they prepare. This creates bonding time and builds their self-confidence and sense of responsibility. They come to value and appreciate the time and effort you put forth when cooking since they see firsthand what it takes. I recall one summer morning my sister and I woke up to our very own personalized breakfast on the table made by my eight-year-old daughter and seven-year-old son. Our oatmeal was not only topped with fresh blueberries, it was also inscribed with our first initial, and there was a lovely breakfast note on the table made just for us. Now tell me what parent wouldn't appreciate that with a huge grin on their face!

Give your kids the same grace God has given you. We are all children of God—yes, even us now as adults. How many times have you messed up as an adult, at either work or just in your role as a parent? Did God come down on you every single time, or were you given grace many times?

Kids will be kids and will do mischievous things, even though we have taught them good from bad. Sometimes their intentions are in the right place, but their execution is completely off. Parenting has given me patience. Consider this story where my son's intentions were in the right place, but the execution was not in alignment with his heart.

I came down to the kitchen one morning to discover a mess: chocolate was everywhere, as were cracker crumbs and candy pieces! As it turned out, he had gotten up before me to make me a surprise gingerbread house. He used the saltine crackers as the walls, the chocolate as glue, and the candy as décor. Now, I could have gotten all upset for the mess and the fact he used the expensive chocolate for his creation, but I smiled instead and was grateful for my gingerbread.

Moments like these will uplift your spirit. I even created a "laughing jar" to remind me of all the silly things my kids do. It's a jar with little notes in them describing a funny moment I shared with them. Before you know it, we're going to be left with just memories.

When I took the Single & Parenting Class at my local church while living in Northern California, there was a quote in the video segment we were watching that I'll paraphrase here: "Parent each child and situation uniquely – if the only tool you have in your parenting toolbox is a hammer, every single situation will look like a nail to you."

Becoming a parent is a form of personal development and leadership. When we learn the techniques to deal with the type of person or child we have—their strengths and weaknesses, how they learn, how they interact with others, etc.—these skill sets are also transferable in your business. In business we deal just with grown-ups (or maybe some grown-ups are still kids), but when you know how to identify characteristics and behavioral types, it will enhance your interaction and influence with people.

Do you exercise patience, love, compassion, understanding, and forgiveness, or do you attack everything from an authoritative state?

Set age-appropriate expectations and consequences. Let them decide. Good choices lead to rewards; bad decisions lead to consequences.

In the Love & Logic Parenting course, it is taught to put the emphasis back on the child to help foster their decision making and learning by reflecting on their own behavior. This empowers them more instead of them just observing the parent's reaction to every situation.

In addition to loving and nurturing our children, equipping them with life skills in areas such as self-awareness, health and wellness, financial literacy, and social responsibility will provide them with the tools and skills they need to have a fulfilled life. It may not give them total immunity toward poverty, abuse, joblessness, and other corruption in the world, but it will at least be in their life toolbox to use.

Parenting teaches leadership skills. Leadership isn't just about giving instructions, it's about teaching why those instructions were given so that one day the child-student will know how to apply what they learned without the parent/leader, so that they can also pass it on and teach it. As you can now see, this principle can easily be transferable to your relationships and business. A great leader knows how to effectively teach—not just preach—instructions.

Learn what motivates your children. Learn what their strengths and areas of improvements are and integrate that in how you parent each child. For example, if you have a child that's more visual than auditory, which approach would be most effective when it comes to getting them to perform a task such as cleaning their room—constantly repeating to them to clean their room or helping them create a visual reward chart that lists their responsibilities? I would recommend the latter. This engages them in the activity, and there's a sense of appreciation.

They may be able to communicate this to you, but kids instinctively feel when their parent takes the time to try and understand them and help them. Parenting is about teaching children. It's about equipping them with the thought process and life skills they will need. We are to cultivate and help develop their character. Being a parent is not just about giving instructions. If we are to just give instructions that they simply follow, what's to be done when we are not able to provide instructions at a given moment, situation, or circumstance?

With more women in the workforce, this changes the dynamics of the roles in the household. More men are now involved with housework and caring for children.

Parenting itself is a huge responsibility, but additional,

various family dynamics can present more challenges. I was in a parenting course at my church, and one day we touched on the topic of children having to live in two different homes if the parents were divorced. Children often find it difficult to "be citizens of two governing households." One household had their routine and rules while the other had their own. From what I have learned as a single parent, children need structure and stability for a sense of security and comfort. It's also difficult for the child if the parents are not getting along and are at war with each other; this puts them in a "POW" (prisoner of war) position. An African proverb states, *When elephants fight, it is the grass that suffers.*

I recall one Thanksgiving Day standing in the kitchen of my friend's home (she too was once widowed), and she said to me, "You've been too busy to just grieve." I just stopped and looked at her for a moment, thinking, Who else is supposed to take care of all these responsibilities if it wasn't me?

Although there are similar behavioral patterns in grieving, everyone goes through the cycle on their own time with uniqueness; this can be a separate book by itself.

My friend's question led me to ask myself, Do we fill our plates so full so that we don't have to deal with other stuff?

When it comes to parenting, relationships, or managing our other roles, there is a correlation at the root of behavior tied to how "busy" we are. What I'll be discussing here is not about the social interaction aspect of avoidance; we'll be covering (or uncovering) why we avoid certain tasks.

We associate every particular situation or experience we have with an emotion of pain or pleasure. Whether we are performing a task at work, engaging in a recreational or leisure activity, having a conversation, cleaning, going on a diet, or even sitting still doing absolutely nothing but daydreaming at the sky, we tie that experience to a painful emotion or a pleasurable emotion. This emotional attachment that we each create can often lead to how we develop the avoidance behavior. Have you ever had a task that had priority, yet you just put it on the back burner to avoid it— you ended up being so "busy" and did something else? This usually signals that there's an emotional attachment to a situation that you're trying to pacify.

Pacifying could look like procrastinating—not doing anything at all to address the matter—or it could look like you are doing something to fill the void to replace it. You're trying to replace the feelings or emotions with a more desirable one.

A simple analogy would be at a particular time on one weekend I was to take care of the monthly bills. I must have spent hours constantly reminding myself to get the bills done when in reality I was avoiding the drudgery of the task. When I finally ended up doing the bills, it took only fifteen to twenty minutes at most, and I even recall telling myself, "That's all it took? I spent more time avoiding it!"

This is a basic example of how we can easily avoid simple tasks in life, but what about those bigger items on our plate that impact other people by our actions or lack of actions? Is there something as a parent you're avoiding? Is there something you're avoiding with your spouse or your work? Ask yourself how and why you've associated the emotion of pain with a particular situation. Was it fear—fear of rejection, fear of loss, fear of success, or maybe fear of inadequacy?

Speaking for myself, one of my business coaches put me on the hot seat and peeled back my layers of avoidance. It was like peeling an onion and having to sit there with watery eyes. It was during a time when I felt like I wasn't ready yet to speak more about my story in front of audiences. My excuse was that I wanted to get everything perfectly ready: my website needed updating, my speech topics needed to be all written out, and my program initiatives needed to be polished (that right there should have been my own red flag since this is a living document that constantly gets updated and refined—it's never going to be finished).In reality, I had everything I needed to just get out there and speak. My fear was speaking, but the fear was rooted in self-sabotaging thoughts of inadequacy. This is when I realized that *I am the perfect example because I am not perfect*. People don't relate to perfectionism because it's unrealistic. (This is not the Spirituality section where we defend that we are perfect images of our Creator.) When I say "perfect" in this example, I refer to our choices and actions.

What is your fear and how have you been avoiding it? Instead of focusing on the pain of fear itself, focus on the future benefits that will come once you accomplish your task. Or if you're a sadistic person, focus on the pain that it will bring if you don't complete the task. This goes back to what was covered in the personal development section on how our perceptions and the neuropathways to our brains shape and condition our beliefs.

I know someone that is preoccupied with an inaccurate magnification of their insecurities or shortcomings, and they've relied on their avoidance behavior as a survival tool because of their fear of rejection or loss.

When we avoid something, pacifying gives us an escape and brings relief as a way of interrupting the painful thoughts of our discomfort.

What I have learned is that we oftentimes magnify our pain association to a point that's not even realistic. You'll probably find yourself saying, "That wasn't that bad after all" after you've challenged your fear.

If you're an overachiever, perfectionism can be a crutch. Or maybe you've caught the Alpha-Mom Syndrome.

(http://www.huffingtonpost.com/beth-rosen/battling-the-alpha-mom-syndrome_b_3844828.html

http://www.examiner.com/article/alpha-female-syndrome)

The Alpha-Mom is the mom that can and does do it all—from having a full-time career, volunteering at school functions, being president of the PTA, baking cookies with her kids, mowing the lawn, cooking, cleaning, taking care of the hubby, paying the bills online while talking on the phone, and running with the family dog around the neighborhood (and probably with a baby jogger too). Sounds exhausting, doesn't it? Why do women overcompensate? There are several elements that play into the role of an Alpha-Mom. Is it the fear of inadequacy, the attempt to control what's controllable, being a people pleaser who is unable say no, being naturally nurturing, being a single parent in survival mode, being competitive, or does it go back to the avoidance behavior?

Through our own learnings from trials and errors, I encourage parents to constantly ask themselves, *"What footprints do we want to leave behind for our kids to follow?"*

"The dynamics and complexities of parenting may present challenges, but it is truly a blessing."

"A great leader knows how to effectively teach, not just preach instructions."

CHAPTER 6

Love & Relationships

———————— ≈ ————————

What do love and relationships have to do with having a healthy mind, a healed body, and a happy soul? Actually, all the topics we previously discussed—overcompensating, health, spirituality, parenting—share the common denominator of love.

Everyone experiences love differently and has various thermostats to gauge love. One might describe love as the affection toward another person, an admiration, a state of mind, but my favorite is unselfish loyal and benevolent concern for the good of another (Webster.com).

I believe that even though love can be given and received, it is already within us—it just needs to be nourished to grow. This brings up the topic of "nature vs. nurture." I do believe that our upbringing and environment influence our human traits, behaviors, and the shape of our lives. However, the dominating force that determines who we are and who we become is what's inside of us (who we naturally are)—we simply choose what to nurture. Whatever you nourish is going to grow. If you keep focusing on the negative and hanging around a negative environment, it's most likely going to be a challenging effort to thrive.

L (Lives within us)

O (Optimistic)

V (Value)

E (Everlasting)

I am not a counselor or a therapist, but I do speak from a different place of authority based on real-life examples.

Overcompensating

Is love part of the element that gives us permission to overcompensate or even to compromise?

I don't think we overcompensate or compromise because we lack self-love; I think it has more to do with the fact that we will do more for others than we do for ourselves.

"We Cultivate love when we allow our most vulnerable and powerful selves to be deeply seen and known, and when we honor the spiritual connection that grows from that offering with trust, respect, kindness, and affection. Love is not something we give or get; it is something that we nurture and grow, a connection that can only be cultivated between two people when it exists within each one of them-we can only love others as much as we love ourselves. Shame, blame, disrespect, betrayal, and the withholding of affection damage the roots from which love grows. Love can only survive these injuries if they are acknowledged, healed, and rare." – from

Brene Brown's *Daring Greatly*

Health & Wellness with Spirituality

Love is so powerful that we underestimate its strength and meaning. One of my secret learnings in adversity is not only allowing forgiveness but finding the strength to overcome. The secret is knowing where and what the strength is—it is the love in our hearts. Do we love ourselves enough? Do we love our bodies enough to treat and value our health? Many illnesses and diseases can be cured naturally by letting the body heal itself. Science even shows that when a patient undergoes a heart transplant, the two hearts are synchronized in beats naturally just by placing one heart on top of the other. Other studies have shown how couples in love can have matching heartbeats, even when they are observing the other loved one in a stressful situation such as fire-walking.

http://news.nationalgeographic.com/news/2011/05/110504-fire-walking-hearts-beat-science-health-heartbeats/

http://news.ucdavis.edu/search/news_detail.lasso?id=10494

Also, recall from the Health & Wellness Section the 528 frequency of love that heals. Love is the fundamental essence of how we were created—with love and out of love from our Creator.

"I can do all things through Christ who strengthens me"
Philippians 4:13

Parenting

Love bonds the safety, security, and joy between the

parent and child. Children who are loved and nourished reflect this in their development as well as the development of the brain itself. Regions in the brain that affect learning, memory, and emotions are impacted by love. This also goes back to the controversial topic of nature versus nurture. Again some believe we behave according to our genetic dispositions (nature) while others believe our behavior is related to what we are taught (nurture). I believe it is a combination of all the influences of our environment, medications/chemicals we introduce to our bodies, genetic inheritance, the core of our creation, but most importantly what we choose to nourish. Picture a fruit garden. If there were no seeds to plant in the fertile soil that was receiving proper nourishment of light and water, what will grow? Nothing! If I were to say that my upbringing and environment influenced and impacted me completely, I would probably be another statistic of violence, drug abuse, depression, suicide, and whatever else people use as excuses as a victim.

"Can you push play with this movie called Life? Some are pushing rewind to the past or fast-forward into the future."

Relationships

What do we overcompensate or even compromise when we have our rose-colored glasses on that we call "love"?

When we are in the state of love, is it the chemistry of our psychology that allows us to even make compromises?

Have you ever observed anyone madly in love when they are just on Cloud 9 wearing those rose-colored glasses? They seem to glow. They seem to have a buffer or a filter to either see beyond their loved one's flaws or not even see them at all. Lovers can talk all night until the sun rises; share revealing thoughts and experiences; go across country by train, plane, and a boat to see each other; act like little kids playing; and even when they are not physically together, you see them dazed out with a smile.

Wearing these rose-colored glasses can allow us to put our own worth and value behind the shades. Wearing these glasses puts us in a chemically induced state where our psychology makes it okay to accept things that are really not true (if brought out of the shade and held against what we truly value). On the other hand, it allows us to also see past the other flaws in our partner that may seem bothersome but not detrimental to the foundation of the relationship.

Love has a language of its own with various dialects. Do you know your own love language and your partner's? You can take the love language profile from Gary Chapman, author of *The 5 Love Languages*. We speak all five of them, but we each have a primary language:

1. Words of Affirmation
2. Quality Time
3. Receiving Gifts
4. Acts of Service
5. Physical Touch

"Meeting my wife's need for love is a choice I make each day. If I know her primary love language and choose to speak it, her deepest emotional needs will be met and she will feel secure in my love. If she does the same for me, my emotional needs are met and both of us live with a full tank." (*The 5 Love Languages*, Gary Chapman, p. 136)

I love this quote because it shows that love is given genuinely without an expected return; it's a choice, not a "horse trade." Love may be complex, but it should flow organically and seamlessly. After all, wouldn't you want to receive love out of desire as opposed to obligation? A particular scenario that I've personally experienced can be misinterpreted as "conditional" love when one expresses their pain in a form of rejection from love. When you allow yourself to give your heart from love, you may not expect to receive the same love back, but this does not make us immune to the pain when the person doesn't even accept it. One of my mentors Berny Dohrmann once said, and I'll paraphrase, *"You have to allow yourself to be able to receive because you are depriving the other person the gift of giving."* In this case, I was on the giving end.

It's a choice to fulfill a commitment in a bond between two people. The energy can't be denied since it's a natural emotional need that has to be met. Oftentimes two people do really love each other, but they don't understand that they are vibrating at different frequencies and speaking different love languages.

Love takes patience, compassion, dedication, time, effort, perseverance, nurturing, honesty, and an awareness of your own inner being and forgiveness. With what I've learned, love will deliver to conquer and save—through any challenges or adversities—because it stems from the root or core of our being. It is how and why we were created. God created all beings out of love. Without love, there would be no joy, there would be no peace, there would be no hope, there would be no inspiration, there would be no light; therefore, there would be no life.

When creating the logo for my nonprofit empowering women and youth "Joy's G.I.F.T. (Global Illumination Foundation Thrives)," I wanted it to represent the male and female energy blending in cohesion for growth, clasped together by hands to hold the bond of unity with the shape of a heart to illuminate its love and light globally for Joy's G.I.F.T. You can view the logo on the website for Joy's G.I.F.T.

How do you GIVE and RECEIVE love?

Is the way we "give" love the same way we expect to "receive" love? For example, if your primary language of receiving love is through quality time, do you also give love through quality time? Obviously, when you're in a relationship, it's about learning your partner's language so that you can give in that form, but maybe we have a natural default setting? I often wondered if our languages change throughout our phases in life, and I observed that with my own experience. We have a natural default language, but we often switch to accommodate shifts in our situations. My default love language is quality time. However, after becoming a widow, I noticed that I my love tank in the "receiving gifts" was empty. I didn't understand it at first since I typically wasn't the materialistic type, but then it finally came to me that it was my late husband that showered me with gifts throughout the year. Now that he wasn't around, that part of the "love tank" was depleted. Another example you can think of is what if you're not the "physical touch" type, but you were deeply saddened by some news? The power of a hug may speak louder than any other language at that particular moment.

Why is love important to understand? Love is tied to the fundamental need of being appreciated. I remember when my daughter was only six or seven years old and she said, *"Love can inspire your heart."* We all seek love, but not all of us really know how to describe love or even experience true love. A huge portion of this difficulty is that we each have our own flavor and taste regarding what it is. The purpose of love is to give it unconditionally, meaning without expectation of anything in return. But you can't give it if you haven't nourished it. It is a choice you make to give for the benefit of the well-being of the other individual. It's a powerful choice, and sometimes it comes with a price when our love comes with the pain of rejection, loss, or betrayal.

Losing love can come in different forms, through a death, divorce, or a breakup. However it's inflicted, the trauma it causes can lead to anxiety, stress, and even depression because the neuropathways in the brain that produced all those euphoric emotions are etched. When the pathways get deprived, it creates a hormonal imbalance.

"Grief is not a sign of weakness, nor a loss of faith, it is the price of love." –author unknown

When I experienced pain from love, it was reassuring to hear such a profound validation from Wendy Darling who is an expert in sound healing therapy and created Healing Harmonics. Her statement was, *"God wouldn't put something (love) deeply rooted in your heart if it wasn't meant for you to have, God's not like that."*

The power of love and its healing wellness properties continue to inspire all these scientific studies.

The article "Five scientific studies that show love really is a wonder drug" highlights five benefits of the potency of this four-letter word.

1. Love releases feel-good hormones: In a study conducted at Stanford University, *"When someone is in love, the brain releases endorphins, which give people a sense of euphoria,"* says neuropsychologist Dr. David Lewis, author of *Impulse: Why We Do What We Do Without Knowing Why We Do It*. *"Dopamine is associated with*

optimism, energy and a sense of wellbeing. Because you feel good about yourself and are optimistic, then you are less likely to do things which are self-destructive like drinking too much or smoking. Being in love almost acts as a protection against the bad things in life."

2. Depression: From UC San Diego, Dr. Kai MacDonald studies oxytocin. The power of a hug has shown remarkable increases in oxytocin in the blood. Oxytocin is a hormone released from the brain by touches, hugs, or when a mother bonds with a baby. Oxytocin is being studied to see how it can assist with depression, anxiety, and mood disorders.

3. Relationships and longevity: Dr. John Gallacher's research from Cardiff University shows that there have been positive trends in health and well-being when people are in committed relationships. I think this just means that people tend to live nondestructive lifestyles that create a healthy relationship. It's what the couples are doing with and for each other; it's not simply the act of getting married. Otherwise, why is the divorce rate so high?

4. Bad relationships weaken your immune system: Dr. Janice Kiecolt-Glaser and Dr. Ronald Glaser spent three decades studying how stress affects immunity. Weakening your overall immune system causes you to become ill. Having toxins or toxic relationships impacts your mental, emotional, and physical state.

5. Lowering stress: Jay Brewer, head of physiology at Nuffield Health, quotes a study by the American Journal of Cardiology that says when focusing on positive thoughts such as appreciation and love, a person's heart rate variability (HRV) increases (which is good). HRV measures the time gap between heartbeats, and it's an indicator for how the body is responding to stress. Brewer says high HRV reduces blood pressure and improves the immune system and

digestion. Having low HRV results in increased levels of adrenaline and cortisol, which is how we get into "fight or flight" mode. Being in this mode can lead to cravings for sugar and fatty foods, a lack of sleep, and weight gain. Having our ecosystem of health in this state is not sustainable; blood sugar levels, energy levels, mental focus, and our emotions are compromised.

Now that you've seen the research on love and how it affects your health and relationships, are you evaluating yours as you read this?

With any relationship, whether it's business or personal love, there's always an exchange of meaning and value. One way to determine what the other person values is to observe what drives their emotional response.

In the Parenting section, we covered the topic of how we associate meanings to a circumstance that causes an emotional response in us. Two people could be sitting in a movie theater watching the same movie and they could have different reactions to a scene based on their own emotional interpretation; one person may seem sad while the other person doesn't. Our emotions allow us and others to tell what's in our hearts.

"Wherever your treasure is, there is the desires of your heart will also be" (Matthew 6:21).

This means whatever you value and treasure is going to trigger an emotional response. Here are a few examples:

• If you treasure love, what would your emotional response be if you lost love?

- If you treasure the security of money, what would your emotional response be if you lost your job, your business wasn't growing, or you couldn't cover your expenses?

Observe yourself and see what type of emotional response you would have. You can also observe where your partner's heart is. If their heart treasures money and they have placed a high value on it, all you have to do is follow their actions regarding where their money goes. They will know exactly how much is in each account, they won't foolishly spend it on "junk" items, and they will give money to those persons they also value. If a person treasures helping people, follow where they spend their time. They will put other people's needs in front of their own, people will gravitate to them for help, they will volunteer at charities and/or churches, and they will oftentimes become the family mediator.

In addition to observing an emotional response, you can also gauge someone's character by observing how they operate during an adversity or under pressure; is the person able to control their emotions, are they able to rationalize to make a decision (as best as possible), do they rely on their faith, do they believe that they can call upon an infinite intelligence for assistance, do their preserve humility and rid their ego to call upon others for help? The opposite of all this would be someone who just shuts-down, becomes angry, looses their belief and faith, and puts up a defensive wall and becomes totally negative…this just allows an environment and entry point for evil to not only take a person's free-will but the capacity to even know the difference.

Mastering your emotions is vital to rising above life's challenges. Notice the "-ing" at the end of the word "master." I did not write "master-ed" as if you've completed perfection because it is always progressing. Have you ever noticed that certain things that used to bother you when you were younger seem so miniscule now? Well, our emotional perceptions have changed and progressed.

Recognize your emotions, but go with what you really know—not what you feel. This is living by faith and not just feelings. When it comes to love, we use our compass for joy and happiness, but if that compass is not calibrated and pointing to the True North, your happy-go-lucky feelings will take you to a place of disaster and disappointment. When you live by faith and go with what you know, you know that God will always stay true to his promises—just follow faith. Maybe that's why faith is blind because if it came with feelings, our feelings could lead us in the wrong direction.

Remember, there's a difference between recognizing our emotions and living our emotions. If someone broke into your home, should you curse at all your neighbors because you're upset?

I'm sure you've heard before that forgiveness allows for healing and progress to transpire. Has someone ever said they forgive you, yet their actions toward you seem to say they have not forgotten? When you speak forgiveness unto someone or a situation, it is not forgiveness by itself that gives grace—it is love. The essence of love is what breathes life into forgiveness. Love allows forgiveness to take place first before transformation.

You might be wondering how to forgive someone who has done you wrong if you don't love them. Well, I have good news for you—you don't. I didn't say love the person you are forgiving; I simply stated that the essence of love is what breathes life into forgiveness. Do you love yourself enough to remove yourself from a toxic relationship? Do you love God enough to trust the faith he blessed you with and to follow? Do you love others around you who are suffering because your ego doesn't know forgiveness? Forgiving can be difficult because when we have been wronged, it is the ego's job to protect us (to an extent), and we revert to a defensive mode. When we do forgive, what happens? We have freedom because oftentimes it is ourselves that we don't release from the pain, anger, and resentment.

True biblical and godly forgiveness is this: *"God shows his love for us in that while we were still sinners, Christ died for us"* (Rom 5:8) and *"while we were enemies we were reconciled to God by the death of his Son, much more, now that we are reconciled, shall we be saved by his life"* (Rom 5:10).

The Greek word for "enemies" is literally "hated, hateful, hostile," and "opposing," so forgiveness is dying for someone while they still "hated or were hostile" toward you. That is what God calls forgiveness. We all hated God before we were saved because Paul writes that *"while we were still enemies"* of God, he *"died for us."*

(http://www.patheos.com/blogs/christiancrier/2014/06/22/top-7-bible-verses-about-forgiveness/#ixzz3CHyZddAZ

Anthropologist Helen Fisher studies gender differences and the evolution of human emotions. She is known for her expertise in love and gave a talk on TED. She describes the brain system that has to do with love; it is lust, romantic love, and attachment.

Around sixteen minutes into the talk, she says, *"But these three brain systems: lust, romantic love and attachment, aren't always connected to each other. You can feel deep attachment to a long-term partner while you feel intense romantic love for somebody else, while you feel the sex drive for people unrelated to these other partners. In short, we're capable of loving more than one person at a time. In fact, you can lie in bed at night and swing from deep feelings of attachment for one person to deep feelings of romantic love for somebody else. It's as if there's a committee meeting going on in your head as you are trying to decide what to do. So I don't think, honestly, we're an animal that was built to be happy; we are an animal that was built to reproduce. I think the happiness we find, we make. And I think, however, we can make good relationships with each other."*

Toward the end, around eighteen minutes, she says that the world would be a dangerous place without love, and here's how she unpacked the science behind that statement. Over 100 million prescriptions of antidepressants are written every year in the U.S. Serotonin enhancers in the antidepressant cause a decrease in dopamine. Dopamine is associated with romantic love and the lust/sex-drive part is also affected. When the lust is essentially killed, there is no orgasm to create the chemicals in the brain associated with attachment.

Fisher's studies and continued work profound discusses all the topics we've covered, including health, love, relationships, women in the workforce, and our roles both in the workforce and at home. It's interesting to see that both Dr. Horowitz's and Fisher's work from different fields of study all converge on the common denominator of love. For me, it's validating and confirming to know that I learned something in my adversities. When adversity presents itself, you're forced to take the fast track in the survival lane to learn while others study it as their profession as well as teach it to others.

A true love story never ends. Because I grew up in an abusive childhood environment, you may assume that I didn't believe in love. I had the blessing of accepting love when my late husband came into my life during one of the most pivotal phases in my life. He was able to see me, the real me, hidden inside that was too insecure to grow. He provided the comfort for my security, the light to foster my growth. He saw past my flaws.

Our relationship taught me to be the woman I am today, the mother to my children, the wife I was, and the wife I will once again be.

He was able to show me what love looked and felt like. Now I am able to share this blessing with others.

If you came from or still are in an unhealthy and abusive environment/relationship, you have my permission to borrow my trust and belief that there is love for you—and also within you, given by the grace of God. You may not believe this at this particular moment in your life, and how can anyone blame you for thinking this? Your perception is your reality, the reality of the now of what you see, hear, feel, and experience. Allow someone to reach out to you to help you or reach out for help.

If you've experienced love and lost it, it's so powerful for you and others to share that blessing. Share your story by telling it, writing it, or giving it. The love you were granted still lives within you. Amplify it by sharing it.

Many people seek to be loved, accepted, and understood. You were blessed with yours, so if you give the gift to someone else, you'll feel the power of its beauty. I learned from one of my mentors that everyone wants to be understood, but once they take time to understand, then they will be understood.

It took me about three years after becoming a widow to start entertaining a relationship in my life again. It would never be fair to me, my late husband, and this new person in my life to try to replicate who my late husband was and expect this new person to be the same. I respectfully accept both are different. I did want to replace the feelings of emptiness, sadness, and loneliness with feelings of fulfillment, happiness, and love again. With what I have learned and evolved to as a woman and mother, it has made me a better person (not perfect—better),being able to come from a place of unselfishness and pure, genuine love and to give from that space. All that was given to me, so I share and spread my joys and blessings through love.

So what did love look like for me during this new phase of my life? I would describe this survival mechanism within me that was love itself. You see, I was humanly ready to have companionship with another person, to be connected and loved, but I believe subconsciously there was a layer of protection for my safety. It was as if my being was protecting me from having to go through another form of death or loss.

The relationship had to be "safe" for me. Coming out of such a traumatic experience, I didn't need something else to rewind me back. Let me explain: The relationship wasn't orthodox to my standards, and those who know me would probably question my positioning. Somehow this survival mechanism layer combined with rose-colored glasses made it okay to not only accept the other person's flaws (which is what we should do when we love someone), but I also allowed his sins to become my own. He was very transparent from the beginning regarding his struggles to commit to relationships. But you see, the unorthodox dynamics worked for me at that given time. The relationship provided what I wanted—fun, connection, companionship—but I didn't need to be in a serious relationship to risk the trauma of rewinding through another loss. I wasn't fully emotionally healed, so it was safe.

Besides the human default protection, which took me some time to realize with the help of one of my energy/transformational coaches, I was still genuinely operating and giving from a place of love, so was this a compromise? To be able to give love right past someone's flaws and see whom they were really meant to be? This was given to me in my marriage, so I was able to gratefully give it to the person I was sharing my love with.

There came a time when the survival piece was being worn down by the thriving piece. I started to reassess my values, my integrity, my health, my worth, and my time. Why did love allow me to compromise so much? That saying is true: you can never change other people, only yourself. So the way I see it, make a change to see a change! There could be effort and intentions for changing, but actions need to be in alignment with those efforts and intentions to result in change.

"No one can change the law of hypnotic rhythm any more than one can change the law of gravity, but everyone can change himself....in all the discussion of this subject that all human relationships are made and maintained by the habits of the individuals related" in Napoleon Hill's *Outwitting The Devil, The Secret to Freedom and Success.*

I was being sensitive to both sides of the relationship and wanted to know if I brought meaning and value into this person's life. Nothing really is new under the sun because after I went through all this, I finally read in Gary Chapman's *5 Love Languages* where he speaks on the topic of making requests versus demands. When you make a request to your loved one, in essence you are affirming their worth and abilities because you feel secure in their love to provide something that is meaningful and worthwhile. For my particular situation, I constantly asked if I brought meaning and value because I felt like he wasn't making a request—he wasn't "letting me in his personal life."

Once I stopped compromising my worth, my values, my integrity, my health, and my time, the dynamics of the relationship began to transform and evolve.

This relationship challenged me to continually grow, trust, and seek God's divine love and constant comfort. This person and I were alike in many ways, but what I appreciated the most was our differences. It was our differences that enabled each of us to elevate and polish each other's character. Picture someone holding a huge flashlight that's casting a bright beam of light on you. This light creates a shadow representing the your areas or weakness that need light. This shadowy dark area needs the light for nourishment and growth. The foundation of a relationship is critical to its growth and contribution. A strong foundation is built on love.

Sometimes our challenges created doubt in my hopes and desires. Especially after continued disappointments, my confidence and spirit were being conflicted and challenged. I was at a point where I felt like I wasn't valued, trusted, or respected—just denied. It's like looking into the mirror of your other half and the reflection is shattered by rejection, and each shattered piece is pierced into your heart.

What was this predicament of contrast I experienced? Were love and connection enough? I think there's an overriding element that supersedes all—timing. Love expert Helen Fisher may also include proximity as well as timing. I believe that even though you may be right for each other, if the channel of time is off, you'll just cross paths instead of connect paths. I wouldn't want to force a crossing of paths on someone; it's not organic. Some people do this, based on circumstances and situations, but when the path is not fostered organically with time, it's like a crash course for disaster. Like the saying goes, *"If there were more courting in marriage, there would be less marriage in court."* Well, the courting part takes time.

I did question the element of time if the alignment was in our favor. Too much compromising existed, and at some point I had to ask myself, at what cost? My health, well-being, peace of mind, happiness? My advice is don't settle; don't compromise your values and what makes you happy. Everyone deserves what he or she wants and needs. Many fear that letting go comes with resentment, when in actuality, there's self-worth, confidence, and true love to be discovered. First, though, we must get out of our own way.

I had to put the focus on me, on getting me back—my smile, my joy, my life, my purpose. God was calling, the world was waiting, and my kids were cheering. I even sounded like Eric Thomas, the motivational speaker, when I said to myself, "Will the real April J. Ford please stand up!" I don't like people wasting my time because that's something they can't give back.

"Time is the most important currency in life." – Dr. Mike Murdock.

Love allows vulnerability to overcompensate and compromise. But it also circles back to the love within you that needs to be nourished and nurtured first. You cannot give from an empty tank or an empty wishing well. In my situation, I compromised my values and health and the well-being of my peace, happiness, harmony, integrity, and time. I had to put God and me first and not settle for anything less. To me, it felt like an insult and mockery of God if I kept compromising. God has given me so much of his grace and saved me from all my adversities. Why would I continue to position myself for more rubble…just so I can keep asking for his continued forgiveness without learning? No! It was time for me to flourish with happiness and the blessings he had already granted me.

The real compromise was ruining the true divine spiritual connection through both our flaws and weaknesses. This should be honored and respected in a friendship instead. I often called this the "season of separation." My greatest fear was losing the connection of the relationship and facing loneliness, but it was only a matter of time that allowed me to gain the perspective and realization that I was already living this fear. The complexities of the dynamics didn't constitute what I defined as a relationship; therefore, since I was already living my worst fear, I had nothing else to lose by staying true to who I am and what I value.

I am grateful for this person in my life and even the blessings from the adversity it brought. In essence he taught me to appreciate my true worth—who I truly am—by not giving it to me. When something is automatically given to you, you tend not to value its worth or even recognize it, compared to when you must learn on your own. Then you'll truly appreciate its worth and value.

Gratitude allowed me to appreciate this contrast. It gave me hope that love would exist again. The fun allowed life to come back into me again and bring out my smile, and since this person possessed attributes that were my areas of improvement, such as areas in business, I learned immensely. When he allows his compassion to bring out his bright spirit, the ego resides.

What does love really look like, and are soul mates real?

I'm not going to get into the topics of soul mate vs. twin-soul since this can be an entirely new book itself. Besides, there's only one Creator that knows the true definition of how and why he created each and everyone of us. Having the blessing of being married to the perfect husband and father, I know love is real and I know what it looks like. Every person is seeking to be loved, accepted, and understood. When it comes to love, we strive to pair up with the person who will fulfill our every desire and wish on our checklist. (Yes, everyone has one, even if it's in your head and not written down.) Helen Fisher describes this list as our "love map." But the fundamental element that's missing on people's lists (maybe this is why divorce rates are so high) is how your partner will enrich your spirit. There are soul mates and there are partners. Are you willing to settle for a partner or are you seeking to fulfill your spirit? I believe there are relationships we encounter for a reason, a season, and/or a lifetime.

Don't deplete your soul of the nourishment it needs. I learned this the hard way trying to defy nature by just giving all the time. We are energy beings that must be refilled with energy.

Most marriages today are like business contracts, and people compromise for the convenience. There are expected responsibilities for both parties that are to be upheld in an agreed service time like a service level agreement (SLA).Their marriage problems are secretly withheld by a nondisclosure agreement (NDA), and terminating the contract would yield high penalties and fees—and who knows what the fine print reads. Where is the love, intimacy, and growth in this binding union?

Don't look for someone to make you happy; look for someone that can add to your happiness. You have to stay true to who you are and what you value first. When my sister got married, I remember the officiator saying, *"It's not about finding the right partner; it's about being the right partner."* How do you expect to be happy in a relationship if you don't even know what you want and value and what values you bring?

Start by using joy and happiness as your compass. When you've found your soul mate, you'll come across these euphoric feelings and experiences like you're on Cloud 9:

- Inner knowing – you just feel it; you try to sum up words from Webster's dictionary, but they may not be in there.

- See past the flaws – your connection and love for them overpowers or overshadows their flaws.

- Your souls speak through your eye contact – eyes are windows to your soul, and you feel comfortable making eye contact and letting your souls do their own dancing and talking.

- You finish each other's sentences because you have this mental telepathy going on.

- Your energy is intense – uplift your spirit.

- Feeling of Oneness

- Safe/secure to be vulnerable

- You not only bring out the best in each other, but you help mold and polish each other's uncovered gems. (This means the not-so-pretty stuff, like a diamond buried in the dirt. It needs to be discovered, revealed, and polished before you see its true beauty, but it was your mate that knew the value within you before the beauty shined.)

You Are a Beautiful Rose of Love

The pieces or petals that make up love can be complex or maybe even appear fragmented, but when folded together, its beauty is a rose. Imagine yourself being inside a rose bud: you can see only one petal at a time, depending on the fold. But someone looking at it from the outside can see all the petals folded together to form a beautiful rose bud.

How do your own petals look to you? Have you felt and seen the beauty of God's gifts that he's blessed you with? We sometimes find it hard to see the entire rose bud that is ourselves. The petals that make up your rose are your gifts. Share your beauty with us.

Your Life Song

Whatever adversity or challenges you are facing, think of your life as a beautiful song.

A Note That Plays Its Own Tune — But Belongs To A Beautiful Song

Sometimes when we recollect using our mental notes about our lives, it may reflect a difficult tune. But when these tunes are orchestrated together, it plays a beautiful, harmonious song.

A song of divine love, a song of spiritual growth, a song of challenges, a song of reflections, a song of transitioning, a song of transformation, a song of awakening, a song of recognizing, a song of responding, a song of reevaluating, and a song of rebalancing.

"Love Can Inspire Your Heart" ~ *Anaya Ford*

April J Ford

THE 4 R's IN ACTION

April J Ford

CHAPTER 7

Using the 4 R's to Rise above Life's Challenges

———————— ≈ ————————

When creating the 4 R's, (Recognize, Respond, Reevaluate, Rebalance), my goal was to provide a simple, practical, and realistic method for navigating through adversity. It is simply organized in four steps:

1) RECOGNIZE the Rubble that needs to be cleared.

2) RESPOND with a Recovery plan for transitioning from tragedy to triumph.

3) REEVALUATE the plan as you Rebuild in alignment with your new journey for the future.

4) REBALANCE the relationships in your life that give you life.

I will use examples to show how simple it is to use this process to make progress with challenges.

1) RECOGNIZE: In the Risk of Overcompensating chapter, we were able to recognize the symptoms (rubble) of compromise and the price we ultimately pay when we do this.

The symptoms of unrealistic expectations can include feeling overwhelmed and then overcompensating, which results in stress; weight gain; lack of sleep; unhealthy, addictive habits; unhealthy relationships; compromising our own worth and values; compromising our own dreams; depression; anxiety; meltdowns; and dependency on medications.

- Self-assessment: Take the self-assessment at http://www.joysofyah.com/youarenotalonebookgifts

- What does your current equation for happiness, success, and prosperity look like?
  _____

- Which variables of your mind, body, and soul are unbalanced (deficient vs. surplus)?
  _____

Remember this is a self-assessment to benefit you so take your time to answer them honestly and don't cheat yourself, this isn't a competitive exam.

2) RESPOND: Now that we've recognized the rubble, let's respond with a recovery plan. You will start with your health, wellness, spirituality, and then success and happiness. Defining and implementing a plan for success and happiness purposely comes after your health and well-being, this allows for clarity; it's a process of first clearing and cleansing before new ideas and thought patterns are established.

The important thing to remember is to take a holistic approach to provide a balance for the three key variables for your equation: mind, body, and soul.

Recall from the previous chapters: Health & Wellness and Spirituality, the various methods that help with healing such as sound therapy, energy healing, essential oils, crystals, practices such as mediation and prayer, etc..

As you assess your answers from the self-survey, keep in mind these worksheet-type of questions:

Mind:

The mind is a powerful tool. Are you using too much or too little of it?

Ask yourself:

- Am I able to control my own thoughts?
- Do I set goals/have a vision board?
- Do I stimulate my mind by reading, writing, studying, and/or having engaging conversations (not gossip) to exchange thoughts?

Body:

- What do I do to take care of my physical being?(Sometimes we refer to our bodies as our shell.)
- Do I eat consciously healthy? What does "consciously healthy" mean? You can think you are eating healthy by choosing nutritional foods that are known to be good for you—for example, a balanced meal with protein, carbs, fibrous carbs, and low fat—

but do you go beyond that to know how healthy the ingredients really are? Are they organic, pesticide/hormone-free, or overly processed? This is what I mean by eating "consciously healthy."

- How often do I exercise to provide my body with oxygen and to increase my blood flow, building my strength, feeding my muscles, and increasing my endurance and endorphins?

- My body is working twenty-four hours a day even while I sleep. How often do I allow it to properly rest to recover? Many of us already lack sufficient sleep due to daily demands from our jobs, families, and extracurricular activities, and sleep at the end of the day is short changed. Don't let it catch up to you. Physically (externally and internally), this is the secret to the fountain of youth.

- When's the last time I went to the doctor for a physical?

- Have I considered seeing a naturopathic physician?

- Have I considered homeopathic remedies?

- Have I ever had an internal or external cleanse? If so, when was the last time?

- When's the last time I had a spa treatment or therapy or a massage?

Soul:

- Being connected to your soul gives you power to connect within to align with your passion and your Creator. The soul seems to go unrecognized by the majority of people because science unveiled its existence only recently. Even with its progress, the methods used to unveil them are unconventional.

- What goes unnoticed is that the soul is a powerful and integral part of our personal growth. We are able to expand our minds by learning, and we can exercise our bodies, so can we foster our soul for growth. The soul cannot be bought from a university like a degree or exercised at the gym; you just learn from the experience called "life" to find your passion. Find your passion and let it blossom.

• Do I express gratitude? Gratitude is not just about saying "thank you" to another person or just during prayer. Gratitude is an action. It is volunteering with what means you have to give—your time, wisdom, and praise as well as monetary contributions. When you express gratitude, do you just do it routinely as you were trained to have manners? Do you just say "please" and "thank you" because that's what you were taught as a toddler, or did you really say it with meaning? Give yourself a simple gratitude for all your accomplishments, even if those accomplishments are not yet complete. At least you are in process of completing them. Notice I meant self-*gratitude*; it is not to be mistaken with self-*worship*.

• Do I meditate and pray daily?
• Do I have a connection with my Creator?
• Do I express gratitude, love, and joy?
• Do I know what my passions are and what my purpose is?
• What is it that motivates and inspires me?
• Who motivates and inspires me?

Does your plan include a workout regimen, a nutrition plan, a realistic timeline that fits your personality and lifestyle, guidance on how to transition from life events to overcome unexpected obstacles, and help identifying that network of resources that will aid you in achieving your number one goal?

You must have a positive mindset. You must believe in yourself for this transformation to occur. You must have the motivation, commitment, and determination that this will result in a benefit.

Refer back to the self-assessment survey in Step 1, along with the worksheet questions. What does your Mind, Body, Soul balance look like?

Mind: _____

Body: _____

Soul: _____

1) What's in your equation now for happiness, success, and prosperity?

_____

2) What do you want your equation to look like for happiness, success, and prosperity for the next three to five years?

_____

3) Think back three to five years ago. How would you have answered question 2 at that time?

_____

4) Compare your answers in 1 and 3.Are they the same or different? Did you meet your goals? Did they change? Why?

_____

List Your Top 3 Accomplishments:

1)

2)

3)

List Your Top 3 Strengths:

1)

2)

3)

List Your Top 3 Areas You'd Like to Improve:

1)

2)

3)

We can be our own worst critics, but sometimes we should allow people to critique us. Value their expert opinions as long as they are genuinely giving you advice to benefit you and not just putting you down. Most importantly, though, ensure that they are experts whose opinions are worth considering.

Spring Cleaning List:

When formulating a plan, sometimes you have to do what I call "spring cleaning." It doesn't have to actually be spring for you to do spring cleaning in your life. Pull out the weeds in your path, but nourish the blossoms and enjoy it. Identify the weeds as any elements in your life that are hindering your life to flow with progress and happiness. These elements can be stress factors at home or work, unhealthy relationships, bad habits, etc. Do identity the blossoms in your life that bring value and meaning, especially people.

Recognize the people in and around your life that influence you. Identify the good and bad. Foster the relationships that bring value and meaning to you and to that other person.

List the people who inspire you toward your goals or support you:

_____

List the people and/or situations that hinder you achieving your goals (I call this the weeds in your life):

_____

Journal

You should create a daily journal of your activities to not only hold yourself accountable for the goals you are trying to reach but to also act as your blueprint. If you're on an exercise program, write down what exercises you did and how many sets or minutes. If you're on a nutrition program, write out what you ate at each meal. (You can simply start by listing what you ate, or you can be intricate and note it down to the measurements.) If you're trying to pursue a new interest and are still learning about it, write down your research sources and how to obtain them. Once a week you should check in with your wellness/life coach and/or your mentor to keep you on track for your goals.

<u>3) REEVALUATE:</u> Now that you've created a plan, it's imperative to re-evaluate it as you rebuild to track progress.

By the end of a minimum of six to eight weeks, you should reevaluate the plan you created in Step 2. Typically your mind and body need this amount of time to adjust to changes, whether they are changes in your diet, exercise, or just your daily routine. Your journal entries from Step 2 will act as your blueprint to move forward.

With the previous chapter on Defining Success and Happiness, we see that certain life events may change the course of your plans or maybe your definition of what you once thought was happiness and success now changed, this is where the re-evaluating takes place.

Remember—don't give up at this point. Recognize each incremental change and give yourself credit; this is a process. If you are seeing no changes, then your blueprint journal entries will assist you in making the calibrations that need to be made going forward.

Again, do not give up! This is a critical point where people fail and wonder why they are unhappy and unsuccessful. Have you ever written down your New Year's resolution and wondered why, at the end of the year, you end up carrying over the same ones into the following year? It's because you didn't accomplish them in the first place. Did you do any milestone checks throughout the year to review your plans and goals and make calibrations? Or did you just think writing them down at the beginning of the year and asking the universe to grant your wishes by the end of the year would suffice?

Go through these questions with your wellness/life coach and/or mentor:

- What are my goals?
- Was the timeline in my development plan realistic? Was it too lax or was it too aggressive?
- Am I meeting my milestone checkpoints?
- What's motivating me toward those checkpoints?
- What's hindering me from those checkpoints?
- Do I have the motivation, commitment, and determination to be happy, successful, and prosperous?
- Am I being honest with myself in my journal entries?

I've created a special "Companion Journal" to help you along the process and you can download it for free here:

http://www.joysofyah.com/youarenotalonebookgifts/

4) REBALANCE: The relationships in your life that give you life need to be rebalanced. Who brings meaning and value to you, and to whom do you provide meaning and value?

Through our journey and destiny, it's the relationships we have that matters to our foundation of growth. If you're a parent, you have a relationship with you kids, if you are married, you have a relationship with your spouse, if you have a job, you have a relationship with your co-workers, if you have your own business, you have a relationship with your customers and the most important relationship is the one with your creator. Life will have its challenges from health, finances, parenting, successes, spirituality and the path towards self-discovery is being aware of the relationships we connect with through this life time. Do we know which relationships that bring meaning and value to enhance our human and spiritual growth, whom do we contribute to so they are guided towards their growth? We are all here to serve one way or another, nobody is ever alone.

Conclusion

———— ≈ ————

"Every adversity has within it the seed of an equivalent or greater benefit." – Napoleon Hill

In conclusion, if you have read this and you're a mother, wife, sister, career climber, entrepreneur, etc., you now know how to rise above life's challenges with grace, gratitude, love, and joy, and you know that you are not alone. Just as I had divine guidance surrounding me, you do as well. Of course, we can also rely on each other for strength, support, and continued growth.

You have the tools to navigate and rise; this is not a turnkey to get out of challenges. You have the resources and the knowledge to live an empowered life. You have recognized that with all our responsibilities we must learn and manage what's truly important and prioritize our life. What do we compromise, how much, and when? You now know the value of your health and wellness, spiritualty, parenting, love and relationships, happiness, and success. You now know that if you don't put *you* back on your own to-do list, it could lead to a path that causes disruption and eventually destruction. These challenges of adversity can cause mental, emotional, spiritual, and physical pain or conflicts. Women are evolving socially, economically, and spiritually with many demands in the various roles for which we have responsibilities. Many are thriving while others are suffering in silence, and it is up to all of us as a collective consciousness to empower them and let them know they are not alone.

If you are not a woman, you know someone who is that is going through these challenges. You can be the one to tell them that they are not alone and that they too can rise above life's challenges with grace, gratitude, love, and joy.

After becoming a widow, I felt like I went through seasons of contrast. I went from the "cookie-cutter" path of going to school to get my degree, getting married to the perfect husband, having kids, and having money, cars, and homes to the opposite direction when I became a widow. I left my career, got involved in a relationship that was completely opposite of me, sold my home and moved from Northern California to Southern California—away from family and friends—and had no income. In the contrasts of challenges, however, I learned how to appreciate gratitude itself. Rely and reflect on gratitude and you'll see that this is where strength, trust, and faith multiply to increase your belief; then that light will beam brighter.

I felt alone at times in my journey, but we don't have to feel alone because we are not. I learned to ask for guidance and help and you can learn from me. People guided me and HE is always here. Study Napoleon's Hill work especially the Princes of Guidance topic in *Grow Rich With Peace of Mind*, he too reveals we are not alone. At times you may be praying and it seems silent, but you need the stillness and silence to see what's about to transpire. God works miracles in the blink of an eye. At least be able to recognize it to appreciate it when the time is revealed. I have seen and experienced it myself, and this is what increases my faith.

"If God answers your prayer, He is increasing your faith. If He delays, He is increasing your patience. If He doesn't answer your prayer, He is preparing the best for you." –unknown

"I will stand behind you to make sure you don't fall, be there beside you to hold your hand and walk you through it or in front of you to pull you forward."

All my adversities that challenged me have given me the gifts of strength, courage, joy, forgiveness, love, and gratitude. They have enabled me to grow emotionally, spiritually, financially, and overall as a person—as a mother, an entrepreneur, and a philanthropist. In the moment of an adversity, we cannot see past the whirlwind of storms. I would have never thought that becoming a widow would bless me with the many seeds to reap—becoming an awesome single parent, being financially literate and responsible, managing my time wisely, knowing God better, not only learning the alternative wellness modalities but living it, continually growing my spiritual being, fostering love, and creating happiness and wealth...but most importantly, continuing to share and spread my joys and blessings.

Remember—everything in life is connected back to the word *love*. It is how and why we were created. Get to know the healing powers of love and you'll see how it sculpts you. When an artist sculpts a statue, he or she carves away the pieces that weren't meant to be that came from the scars of life's challenges.

You don't have to be a widow to give it everything you've got like the "Widow's Mite."

Mite means coin or money; in the Bible, there was a widow that gave all her mite to Jesus and he valued that more compared to what the others gave. She gave everything she had compared to someone with wealth that gave an amount, which in turn really wasn't a sacrifice. As described in Mark 12:41, *"And Jesus sat over against the treasury, and beheld how the people cast money into the treasury: and many that were rich cast in much. And there came a certain poor widow, and she threw in two mites, which make a farthing. And he called unto him his disciples, and saith unto them, verify I say unto you, that this poor widow hath cast more in, than all they which have cast into the treasury: For all they cast in of their abundance; but she of her want did cast in all that she had, even all her living."* God will see where your heart is, and if you allow him, he will always deliver.

If the Spirituality and Health and Wellness Section aroused some of your skepticism on certain modalities and beliefs, that's okay. I share them because I used to be a skeptic. The engineering part of my brain didn't understand how simple things like breathing, crystals, sound, color, body talk, etc. worked, but when I not only felt but also saw the outcome, and that the outcome matched the results from science, what was there not to believe? Some may describe this as "going off in the deep end". To me, going in the deep end is learning how to swim and living the life we were given, you don't learn by dipping one toe in the kiddie pool.

With what I have learned since my late husband's passing with these other modalities, it would have at least given him a better chance of surviving if we had known.

Use the simple 4 Step 4 R's process: Recognize, Respond, Reevaluate, Rebuild. You will see that you can use this process at any stage of your life with any challenges. I have used it many times to get through a tragedy. Yours might not be as an extreme tragedy, but the process will still work.

First, RECOGNIZE the Rubble that needs to be cleared to start healing. Second, RESPOND with a Recovery plan to transition from tragedy to triumph. Third, REEVALUATE your roadmap as you Rebuild it in alignment with your new journey for the future. Forth, REBALANCE the Relationships in your life that give you life.

"We are all called to do something different, but we are all born with the same grace, gratitude, love, and joy to do it."

There will come a time when it's your turn to be called to fulfill your purpose, and you will be tested. Don't worry about family and friends that don't believe or support you because they don't see your same vision. This is where forgiveness comes in with grace, gratitude, love, and joy. Keep sharing and spreading your joys and blessings.

"There's no greater commitment and responsibility than to honor what's in your heart. It's the voice of your soul."

Favorite Quotes

We are all called to do something different, but we are all born with the same grace, gratitude, love, and joy to do it.

There is always gold to be found in life's challenges; it is the alchemy of adversity.

Every adversity has within it the seed of an equivalent or greater benefit.– Napoleon Hill

Whatever the mind can conceive and believe, the mind can achieve. – Napoleon Hill

You need more than just R&R; you need all 4 R's:

Recognize, Respond, Reevaluate, Rebalance.

My destiny is God's dynasty.

Love can inspire your heart. - Anaya Ford (at age seven)

Share and spread your joys and blessings.

"We are spiritual beings having a human experience." – Pierre Teilhard de Chardin

Can you push play with this movie called Life*? Some are pushing rewind to the past or fast-forward into the future.*

"98% of the population shrink their dreams to fit their income. Meanwhile, the 2% find ways to increase their income so they can make their dreams happen." –Dani Johnson

Your spiritual side is always there. It's like a seed in the dirt, but it needs to be fertilized and nourished in order for it to grow.

The dynamics and complexities of parenting may present challenges, but it is truly a blessing.

My faith is greater than my fear.

What footprints do we want to leave behind for our kids to follow?

A great leader knows how to effectively teach, not just preach instructions.

I can do all things through Christ who strengthens me. (Philippians 4:13)

*Grief is not a sign of weakness, nor a loss of faith; it is the price of love. –*unknown

Wherever your treasure is, there the desires of your heart will also be. (Matthew 6:21)

Time is the most important currency in life. – Dr. Mike Murdock

It's not about finding the right partner; it's about being the right partner.

Stop hitting the snooze button and wake up to your dreams and live them!

Why have you given up on your dreams when the one who created you and gave you those dreams has never given up on you?

If God answers your prayer, He is increasing your faith. If He delays, He is increasing your patience. If He doesn't answer your prayer, He is preparing the best for you. –unknown

I will stand behind you to make sure you don't fall, be there beside you to hold your hand and walk you through it or in front of you to pull you forward.

There's no greater commitment and responsibility than to honor what's in your heart. It's the voice of your soul.

It's imperative to have all three variables of your mind, body, and soul working in cohesion and not opposition; this will give you the traction you need, not friction, to help propel your life with momentum. This is how you THRIVE and not just survive!

"So I say to you, ask, and it will be given to you; seek, and you will find; knock, and it will be opened to you. For everyone who asks, receives; and he who seeks, finds; and to him who knocks, it will be opened." (Luke 11:9)

Don't stand behind your dream to just follow it, LIVE it.

Happiness and success comes from an equation, not a formula.

The soul cannot be bought from a university like a degree, or exercised at the gym; you just learn by experience called "life" to find your passion.

When I look in the mirror, I see confidence and the blessings of my health, but most importantly, when I close my eyes and ask myself what <u>*I feel and see inside*</u>*, I see strength, peace, beauty, and confidence.*

Treat life like a GPS. You must know your desired destination before your turn-by-turn directions. Remember to use your internal compass called intuition as well.

Equations for happiness and success are never set like a formula because the variables change as our life progresses and evolves, so even our own equations will change.

In order to be happy and successful, you must first ask yourself what makes you happy and what your definition of success is.

Don't just survive, THRIVE!

Fear motivates failure.

I hope that the light that I have embraced will radiate to others so that they can share and spread the joys and blessings.

I am not discouraged because every wrong attempt discarded is another step forward.– Thomas Edison

Science without religion is lame. Religion without science is blind.– Albert Einstein

The intuitive mind is a sacred gift and the rational mind is a faithful servant. We have created a society that honors the servant and has forgotten the gift.–Albert Einstein

Nothing will benefit human health and increase the chances for survival of life on Earth as much as the evolution to a vegetarian diet.– Albert Einstein

It's the invisible that creates the visible, the roots create the results of the fruit" T. Harv Ecker

God gave us the code to unlock our DNA for healing…are you operating at the 528 frequency of LOVE?! - April J. Ford

About JoysGift.Org

---≈---

MISSION STATEMENT

Joy's G.I.F.T. empowers widows and abused women-youth on how to transition from tragedy to triumph by providing them with a support system and an infrastructure of resources for services focused on health, healing, and happiness.

Joy's G.I.F.T. (Joy's Global Illumination Foundation Thrives) is a 501(c)(3) women and youth empowerment organization founded by best-selling author April J. Ford who became a widow at the age of thirty-two. The many adversities that April has endured throughout her entire life helped prepare her to deal with the ultimate tragedy of losing her husband in 2010. Lincoln was not only her husband, he was also her best friend and the father of their two young children.

April's passion is dedicated to this global movement to inspire others to overcome adversity through mental, emotional, and spiritual healing.

Joy's G.I.F.T.'s Signature Program:

- 4 Step 4 R's Program – Designed to shorten the road to recovery by delivering an intensive eight-week program. This bridges women to a place of overcoming adversity by finding peace, passion, purpose, and success by studying mindset, health, wellness, and personal development.

About the Author

Who is April J. Ford? She is a best-selling author, entrepreneur, and philanthropist.

April is a purpose driven Entrepreneur that knows the alchemy of adversity and inspires people to find the gold in life's challenges.

April was born in San Francisco, Cal., and was raised in the surrounding Bay Area and Sacramento area. She attended California State University, Sacramento, graduating with a Bachelor of Science degree in Electrical and Electronic Engineering. After being successful in the corporate world for over thirteen years at Intel Corporation, April realized that**her faith was greater than her fear**and walked away as an engineer to fully transition into an entrepreneur.

She has accomplished much in her life, while also overcoming immeasurable hurdles. Her passion fuels her to inspire others to overcome any adversity and to thrive through health, healing, happiness and prosperity.

Learning firsthand the importance of bouncing back from insurmountable difficulties; she lost her husband who was her best friend at thirty-two years young. The many adversities that April has endured throughout her entire life helped prepare her to deal with the ultimate tragedy of losing the father of her two young children in 2010.

She shares her story in*Chase The Challenge and Conquer, My 4 R's: Rubble, Recovery, Rebuild, Relationships,*which was featured on Amazon's Top 100 Best-Seller's List.*Chase The Challenge and Conquer,*along with her Mind, Body, Soul Program titled*4 Step 4 R's; Recognize, Respond, Re-evaluate, Rebalance,* were featured on national TV. These two publications are for you if you're looking to be inspired and empowered to transform into your true potential and if you are looking for practical methods to achieve health, healing, and happiness.

April's brand, J.O.Y. (Joys of Yah), started the vision of how we can all share and spread the joys and blessings from the gifts of life's challenges.

Her dedication expanded to the 501c (3) nonprofit, Joy's G.I.F.T.(Global Illumination Foundation Thrives). Joy's G.I.F.T. empowers widows and abused women-youth on how to transition from tragedy to triumph by providing them with a support system and an infrastructure of resources for services.

Acknowledgements

————— ≈ —————

I thank **God**, my divine creator, for giving me grace and continued love. I vowed that I will obey as you have shown me the way. You have guided me directly, through others and by angels. I know I am not alone. Thank you for allowing me to share my joys, blessings, and gifts. I will continue to seek your wisdom for clarity and guidance as I transform into who you have created me to be. I pray for forgiveness for the mistakes I've made, give gratitude for today, and seek your wisdom for tomorrow.

Anaya & Allen–My little angels. Thank you for supporting Mommy with all my work. I promise that one day you will see the footprints we (you both were by my side the whole time) are leaving behind and really see the blessings God has granted in our path. Always remember Love.

Don Green - I love the stories you share. I gratefully receive the golden nuggets of your wisdom. I know Napoleon

Hill is proud that you have continued to keep his work alive and continue to teach the younger generation his principles. Thanks for your signature in your book with Jeremiah 29:11.

Berny Dohrmann–Thank you for being not only a vessel of wisdom but also for having a heart of generosity. Just as you called Napoleon Hill "Uncle Nappy," I'm honored to have Anaya and Allen call you "Uncle." You hold true to your words when you say, "How can I serve you? What do you need next?"I asked, and I have received. Thank YOU!

CEO Space Business Growth Conference–Keep the spirit alive of fostering an environment of collaboration, not competition. This conference is beyond the normal format of business seminars. It's personal development, spiritually recharging, and where dreams and miracles really do happen. Not everything in Vegas has to stay in Vegas. Share your dreams and miracles that happen at the conference. Thank you Dave Phillipson for shepherding my way.

B.I.G. Collaborative 360 (Bridging Individuals Globally: C-360)–Let's continue to leverage each other's talents and gifts to collaborate. We have so much power in unity to make a positive global impact.

eWomen Network Orange County – Wow! What a welcoming you gave me as I transitioned to my new place called home. With all my gratitude to all the women (a few men) who have stood up to support Joy's G.I.F.T.

Joy's G.I.F.T. Board of Directors– Marina, John, and Louis, you are the team that continues to build this dream. You are the leaders women need when facing a challenge transitioning from their tragedy.

Macio – Thank you for taking the time to really understand me. My love and light for you, always. It is a blessing with gratitude that our paths have crossed. Your spirit is amazing; continue to allow HIM to work through you for compassion, love, and deliverance.

Mark Brown – Thank you for sharing your gifts and stories. You always seem to know which books to recommend to me at the appropriate time as I am seeking certain answers myself. Thank you for that guidance.

Robbin Simons – You Are Not Alone went from pen to publication in sixty days! And in reality, the writing portion was actually thirty days. Continue to push the limits of our beliefs. This project took focus, a strategic plan, and a great team. Thank you for having an integral role in all three.

Secret Knock – Extending my gratitude for accommodating some of the challenges I've had to navigate through being an entrepreneur and a single mom that moved to a new area. You guys are like family and accepted my kids at the events like your own. If all they remember from the event is how fun it is, then all those challenges I had to navigate were worth it.

Sherita Herring – I appreciate all the coaching times that you poured into me. You continue to expand my awareness and creativity. Thank you for being honest when I needed to recognize proper sequence and strategy. You were also integral in creating the proper compliances with the 501c(3) for Joy's G.I.F.T. You're a leader who is dedicated and delivers; I know C-360 is in good hands as we embark on a major global mission.

Tammy Adams – I'm blessed to have learned and grown spiritually from all that you have taught me. You not only have a God-given gift but also the knowledge you've learned from priests, healers, Native American tribes, African tribes, etc. The guidance of your support reflects that I wasn't alone in this process; none of us are. We are truly holistic beings, so we must learn holistic methods of healing. I sit here now writing this at the Mission in San Juan Capistrano, all with praise to God.

Tom Cunningham–Continue to inspire others as a Certified Napoleon Hill Instructor. I'm thankful for the opportunity you gave me when you passed the mic to me to host shows on Journey To Success.

Wendy Darling–As *Forbes* calls you, "Darling Wendy," you are incredibly amazing. Your story of how you literally fell to hit rock bottom then transformed with spiritual freedom to grow speaks volume. Your example shows us that we shouldn't have to wait until we hit rock bottom to be able to listen to our soul speaking to us. Our soul guides us to make our dreams come true. You have a unique "Fairy God Mother" attribute about you with your invisible Love wand that allows the rest of us to dance as you sing to our soul.

Every single person that took the time to read *You Are Not Alone* before it was released, I thank you for your testimonies and reviews on Amazon.

To all my friends, family, and fans (as well as my children's friends) in Folsom, Sacramento, and the Bay Area, thank you for your support during our relocation. We miss you. Know that we are only a thought away.

I hope that the light that I have embraced will radiate to others so that they can share and spread the joys and blessings and have the domino and ripple effects. Allow this awareness and awakening to enlighten you to find freedom in your spiritual path and find your gold in life's challenges.

You Are Not Alone...

April J Ford

In Gratitude to You

Thank you for your generosity in purchasing YOU ARE NOT ALONE. Proceeds will benefit the non-profit Joy's G.I.F.T. empowering women who have experienced a loss such as widows & abused women and youth.

I would be so grateful if you could take a minute or two and provide an honest review for this book on our sales page.

Disclaimer

Please consult with your personal physician, nutritionist, trainer, and/or Wellness Coach before integrating the 4 Step 4 R's Program with your lifestyle as you should with any other program.

Although the methods will work for any individual and during any stage in their life, the specific personal examples/experiences may not be suitable for all audiences. Depending on your level of vibrational operation and consciousness, some methods may seem unconventional and not intended for all audiences.

Ford, April J. *Chase The Challenge and Conquer, My 4 R's: Rubble, Recovery, Rebuild, Relationships.* Bloomington: WestBow Press, 2012.

As with all programs, techniques and materials related to health, exercise, and fitness, the 4 Step 4 R's Program recommends that you not rely upon or follow the programs, techniques or use any of the products and services made available by or through the use of this book for decision making without obtaining the advice of a physician or other health care professional. The information, products, and services made available by or through the use of this book are provided for use by persons who have satisfied themselves as to the appropriateness of its use for themselves after obtaining the advice of a physician or other health care professional. The nutritional and other information in this book is not intended to be and does not constitute health care or medical advice and must not be used to make any diagnosis specific to the user. The 4Step 4 R's Program does not employ dietitians or any other health care professionals.

If you have chosen not to obtain a physician's permission prior to beginning this program with the 4 Step 4R's, then you are doing so at your own risk.

By your use of this book, you acknowledge that you do hereby waive, release, and forever discharge the 4 Step 4R's Program and its respective heirs, directors, officers, agents, employees, representatives, successors and assigns, administrators, executors, and all others from any and all responsibilities or liability from injuries or damages resulting from or connected with your participation in any of the 4 Step 4 R's exercise programs (including any newsletters) whether arising from the negligence of the 4 Step 4R's, its employees, heirs, directors, officers, agents, employees, representatives, successors and assigns, administrators, executors, and other parties involved in the creation, production, or delivery of the site, or otherwise.

Bibliography
Referenced Resources

Books:

Brown, Brene. *Daring Greatly – How The Courage To Be Vulnerable Transforms the Way We Live, Love, Parent, and Lead.*Gotham Books, 2012.

Butler, Tricia. Body Talk. Skype: tricia.butler7

Chapman, Gary. *The 5 Love Languages.* Northfield Publishing, 1992.

Corbin, David M. *Illuminate – Harnessing the Positive Power of Negative Thinking.* John Wiley & Sons, Inc., 2009.

Fay, Jim and Fay, Charles. *Love and Logic Magic for Early Childhood.* Midpoint Trade Books, Inc., 2010.

Ford, April J. *Chase The Challenge and Conquer, My 4 R's: Rubble, Recovery, Rebuild, Relationships.* Bloomington: WestBow Press, 2012.

Hawkins, Jennifer. *The Gift Giver.* Emerald Book Company, 2011.

Johnson, Dani. *First Steps To Wealth.*Call To Freedom Int'l, LLC, 2011.

Hill, Judy. *Crystal Bible 2.*Godsfield, 2009.

Hill, Napoleon. *Grow Rich With Peace Of Mind.* Penguin Group, 1967.

Hill, Napoleon. *Outwitting The Devil , The Secret to Freedom and Success.* Sterling Publishing, 2011.

Wilkinson, Bruce, and David and Heather Kopp. *Dream Giver: Following Your God-Given Destiny.* Multnomah Books, 1984.

Websites:

Adams, Tammy. Crystal Therapy.http://growinginknowledge.com/

Darling, Wendy.Healing Harmonics.http://wendydarling.com/

Horowitz, Leonard. 528 Frequency of Love.http://www.thebookof528.com/TheBookOf528/Hom e_files/The_Book_of_528_e-Edition_Sample.pdf

Wootton, Amy and Douglas, Pamela. "Zyto Scan & Essential Oils." Well Core Network.

http://wellcorenetwork.com/

Attia, Sarah. Somadome. http://www.somadome.com/

4 Step 4 R's Program
http://www.amazon.com/Step-Mind-Body-Soul-Program-ebook/dp/B00DVF5WAY/ref=sr_1_10?s=books&ie=UTF8&qid=1410424678&sr=1-10&keywords=4+step+4+r%27s+program

Worksheets:
http://www.joysofyah.com/youarenotalonebookgifts/

Consultations/sessions, e-mail: apriljford@joysofyah.com

J.O.Y. – Joys of Yah
www.joysofyah.com
Joy's Global Illumination Foundation Thrives (G.I.F.T.) -
Nonprofit for Widows & Abused Women-Youth
www.joysgift.org
Blogs:
http://authorapriljford.com
http://apriljford.com

Videos/Books:
YouTube Videos including ABC Commercial

http://www.youtube.com/joysofyah

Kristen White The Ripple Effect Show, ABC

http://kristenwhitetv.com/

Harry Oldfield YouTube presentation on energy fields

http://www.youtube.com/watch?v=-W45AkDHnsQ&feature=youtube_gdata_player

*Single & Parenting – Hard Work, Real Hope.*Church Initiative. 2011.

http://metro.co.uk/2014/02/13/five-scientific-studies-that-show-love-really-is-a-wonder-drug-4301331/

Referenced Blogs and Extras

———— ≈ ————

Main Blog sites:
http://authorapriljford.com
http://apriljford.com

Blog: Religion and Spirituality, Yoga Is A Religion

http://authorapriljford.com/religion-and-spirituality-yoga-is-a-religion/

Blog: How Can You Tell When You Are Healed

http://authorapriljford.com/how-can-you-tell-when-youre-healed/

Blog: How Fear Motivates Us

http://authorapriljford.com/how-fear-motivates-us/

Blog: There Are Equations For Happiness and Success But It's Not A Formula

http://authorapriljford.com/there-are-equations-for-happiness-success-but-its-not-a-formula/

Blog: Ricochet Back At Life

http://authorapriljford.com/ricochet-back-at-life/

Blog: The Power Of Believing

http://authorapriljford.com/the-power-of-believing/

Website: Scriptures, Holy Bible – YouVersion Bible App

Journey To Success Radio Interviews:

(April with: Dr. John Turner, Sharon Lechter, Dr. Gladys, Tom Sutter, and more)

http://www.joysofyah.com/media-kit/

Applied Faith segment

(Berny Dohrmann, April Ford)

http://youtu.be/UAtV2uPCB5k

www.ingramcontent.com/pod-product-compliance
Lightning Source LLC
LaVergne TN
LVHW021451080426
835509LV00018B/2244